THE PERFECT TRADITION

The Avataric Great Sage,
ADI DA SAMRAJ

THE
PERFECT
TRADITION

The Wisdom-Way of the Ancient Sages
and Its Fulfillment
in the Way of "Perfect Knowledge"

BY

THE AVATARIC GREAT SAGE,
ADI DA SAMRAJ

THE DAWN HORSE PRESS
MIDDLETOWN, CALIFORNIA

NOTE TO THE READER

All who study the Way of Adidam or take up its practice should remember that they are responding to a Call to become responsible for themselves. They should understand that they, not Avatar Adi Da Samraj or others, are responsible for any decision they make or action they take in the course of their lives of study or practice.

The devotional, Spiritual, functional, practical, relational, and cultural practices and disciplines referred to in this book are appropriate and natural practices that are voluntarily and progressively adopted by members of the practicing congregations of Adidam (as appropriate to the personal circumstance of each individual). Although anyone may find these practices useful and beneficial, they are not presented as advice or recommendations to the general reader or to anyone who is not a member of one of the practicing congregations of Adidam. And nothing in this book is intended as a diagnosis, prescription, or recommended treatment or cure for any specific "problem", whether medical, emotional, psychological, social, or Spiritual. One should apply a particular program of treatment, prevention, cure, or general health only in consultation with a licensed physician or other qualified professional.

The Perfect Tradition is formally authorized for publication by the Ruchira Sannyasin Order of Adidam Ruchiradam. (The Ruchira Sannyasin Order of Adidam Ruchiradam is the senior Cultural Authority within the formal gathering of formally acknowledged devotees of the Avataric Great Sage, Adi Da Samraj.)

Produced by the Dawn Horse Press,
a division of the Avataric Pan-Communion of Adidam

International Standard Book Number: 1-57097-197-8

Library of Congress Catalog Card Number: 2006930891

THE "PERFECT KNOWLEDGE" SERIES

THE PERFECT TRADITION

✦ ✦ ✦

RELIGION AND REALITY

✦ ✦ ✦

THE LIBERATOR

✦ ✦ ✦

THE ANCIENT REALITY-TEACHINGS

✦ ✦ ✦

THE WAY OF PERFECT KNOWLEDGE

The books of the "Perfect Knowledge" Series are drawn from
*Is: The "Perfect Knowledge" of Reality and The "Radical" Way
to Realize It,* by the Avataric Great Sage, Adi Da Samraj.

The five books of the "Perfect Knowledge" Series
together comprise the complete text of *Is*.

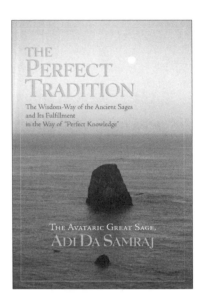

ABOUT THE COVER

Throughout His Life, Avatar Adi Da Samraj has worked to develop means—both literary and artistic—of communicating the True Nature of Reality. He approaches the creation of His literary and artistic works as a process of Revealing What Reality Is and how Its True Nature can be Realized.

For the cover of *The Perfect Tradition*, Avatar Adi Da has chosen a photograph He took in 1998 on the coast of Northern California.

Examples of the artwork of Adi Da Samraj, together with discussions of His artwork and His own statements about it, may be seen online at:

www.daplastique.com

CONTENTS

Introduction to
The Perfect Tradition

by Carolyn Lee, PhD

There is a dimension of existence that is off the edge of the mind. Words can only gesture paradoxically toward it. And yet the most urgent human need is to plumb this dimension, to get to the source of things, to know Reality with a capital "R", in order to make sense of the chaos of experience. This fundamental enquiry was conceived by the author, during His youth, in visual terms:

> *From My early years, including My college period, I would have an image, a visual impression, of a group of people sitting around a massive boulder-like stone in a room. There were no windows, no features to the room at all, no reason to be looking at the room itself. I would be sitting with others, in chairs, around this stone—turned directly at the stone, simply persisting in that situation. There was the sense that eventually everything would be known—meaning Realization would be the case—based on the starkness of that scene. It was about the transcending of the objective by simply looking at what <u>Is</u>—simply the room itself, or the great stone, the mere event of conditional awareness.*
>
> —March 1 and 4, 2006

The primal circumstance of contemplating what <u>is</u> is native to the human being. But who can "explain" what <u>is</u>? Who can answer the conundrum of the stone? What <u>is</u> the stone? Why is there a stone at all? Why does anything arise? What is the Source of all of this happening?

During His childhood, and on into His years at Columbia College, New York, Adi Da Samraj was possessed with the question: "What is consciousness?" By "consciousness" He meant that very sense of existence, or awareness of simply being—that which is constant in us, whatever the events and changes of life. In the modern scientific view, consciousness is the by-product of an electro-chemical process originating in the brain, and, therefore, dependent on the survival of the body. Thus, according to this opinion, consciousness, which seems to be our most fundamental condition, disappears at death. This is the message imparted—even officially—by the institutions of modern "civilization". Avatar Adi Da could never accept it, because He had a greater tacit knowledge, which had been self-evident at His Birth.

Adi Da Samraj was born in New York in 1939 into an ordinary lower-middle-class family—but He was not in an ordinary state. As He describes in His Spiritual Autobiography, *The Knee Of Listening*, He enjoyed in infancy an unbroken Condition of Radiant, Blissful Being, which, from childhood, He has called the "Bright". But He discovered in His earliest years that this sublime Reality was not obvious to others. And so, in a great Impulse to embrace the human condition completely—and, thus, to Illumine it for all—Avatar Adi Da spontaneously relinquished that Native Awareness of Reality. From the age of two, He submitted to participate in the human dilemma, the presumption that one is a separate mortal entity in the midst of a bewildering and threatening world. Nevertheless, the "Bright" persisted as an under-current of Truth that kept driving Him to the root of things—until all obstructions fell away, and the "Bright" was Re-Awakened in Him completely. From that point, He turned about to Teach others.

From time to time in human history, Great Sages have appeared who have, to one degree or another, agreed to instruct devotees. Such a one does not teach from the position of an "I" speaking to "you" or "me". A truly Great Sage speaks as the Very Condition, the Radiant Ocean of Being, That is Reality. Adi Da Samraj, from the beginning of His lifetime, has shown the signs of such a one. He is here in a brief span of a human lifetime, to show that the Ultimate Reality and Truth is not (as He has remarked) a "blank absolute", nor the "Creator–God" (making the world, and implicated in the human drama). Rather, the Very One Who Is, is by Nature moved to Liberate—to set beings free of identification with the sticky web of illusions that makes up the usual life. The Wisdom-Teaching of Adi Da Samraj is a great gift to all who need to understand the human event from the viewpoint of Ultimate Truth, beyond the winds of doctrine and the competing philosophies that have made and unmade the cultures of humankind.

The Great Reality-Teaching Transmitted in Living Relationship

One evening, Adi Da Samraj was seated in His house surrounded by a small group of devotees. He was humorously, compassionately, and lovingly engaging one devotee, Daniel Bouwmeester, in a dialogue—pressing Daniel to inspect the root of the conventional references "us" and "I".

DANIEL: A number of us had questions tonight.

AVATAR ADI DA SAMRAJ: "A number of us"—just what do you mean by that, Daniel?

DANIEL: Individuals. Us.

AVATAR ADI DA SAMRAJ: Are you talking about a real experience of yours—that you are one of something there can be a number of?

DANIEL: Oh, yes.

AVATAR ADI DA SAMRAJ: What is that experience?

DANIEL: Well, it is a sense of there is me and then there are others.

AVATAR ADI DA SAMRAJ: Nonsense! Yes, and what are "they"?

DANIEL: As You have said, there are presumed "others" who are similar to or even the same as myself.

AVATAR ADI DA SAMRAJ: I mean, what is that? What are you referring to?

DANIEL: Generally, other bodies, other entities, but also individuals.

AVATAR ADI DA SAMRAJ: Yes, but you declared yourself to be virtually identical to all these others.

DANIEL: Something similar. "Us" is just a language convention.

AVATAR ADI DA SAMRAJ: So what exactly are you referring to? You cannot just refer to "they are all bodies" because you said you are one of those, and you do not refer to your own body from without. So when you say "I", you mean something different than they mean when they say "you".

DANIEL: Yes.

AVATAR ADI DA SAMRAJ: Well, what is that? Is that what you were referring to when you said "us"? Were you really speaking about yourself, or just using language?

DANIEL: Using language was one part of it, but when You asked me who are the "us", there is just a presumption that there is another person, a physical body . . .

AVATAR ADI DA SAMRAJ: As a convention of speech, yes. But do you mean altogether what you are saying, or do you just <u>use</u> conventions? I mean, are you actually referring to a something when you say "I"?

DANIEL: No. When I refer to the "I", no.

AVATAR ADI DA SAMRAJ: Well, what <u>are</u> you referring to when you say "I"?

DANIEL: The totality of my sense of myself, and also all my experiences as well . . .

AVATAR ADI DA SAMRAJ: But who is the "my", the "me" behind the "my"? Is there a someone other than all those experiences that are remembered?

DANIEL: Yes, yes. I guess it is a sense of essential self, myself. It even seems to be not really definable.

AVATAR ADI DA SAMRAJ: Right now you are referring to it as an "it". But is there a someone other than all those thoughts and memories and such?

DANIEL: Yes.

AVATAR ADI DA SAMRAJ: So what is that?

DANIEL: It is basically just a feeling, a thoughtless feeling.

AVATAR ADI DA SAMRAJ: Yes, yes. You are a thoughtless feeling. It <u>is</u> so, isn't it?

DANIEL: Yes.

AVATAR ADI DA SAMRAJ: But if you just attach yourself to the conventional mind, you think you are referring to what people can observe, or expressions on your face or something "other"—things that are objective to them. But when you examine what you are really referring to as "I", it is a thought-less feeling, as you say. It does not have any mind or body. All experiences of mind and body are objects to it.

The being is, as you say, experientially a thoughtless feeling. Therefore, if you simply feel yourself as such, as you are, what can you say about it? Is there anything else to be said about it, other than "it is a thoughtless feeling"?

DANIEL: It also feels radiant. There is a sense of radiance, but it is not limited by the body. It is not limited by thought or any of the other objects associated with the body.

AVATAR ADI DA SAMRAJ: Do you feel that every being here represented by their bodies is a different thoughtless feeling than you are?

DANIEL: I do not know if I can answer.

AVATAR ADI DA SAMRAJ: What do you <u>feel</u> about it? If you didn't just <u>look</u> at them and focus on them as individuals or <u>think</u> about them, but are just here among them—so-called "them"—do you feel yourself to be a separate thoughtless feeling? Or the same thoughtless feeling that all could refer to?

DANIEL: The same—because when I want to limit it, it seems to be greater than that.

AVATAR ADI DA SAMRAJ: But as soon as you start using the faculties to perceive everyone, not only do you see lots of bodies and suggest separate persons but you begin to create a whole complex of associations and presumptions based on that. In other words, you abandon the position of the thoughtless feeling, and your knowing is all about these perceptual and conceptual complexes, which are otherwise simply Witnessed by you.

If you are to <u>maintain</u> that thoughtless feeling-being, unagitated, how would you live differently—since presently *all of your thoughts and feelings and actions and perceptions are a kind of <u>invention</u> that is dissociated from your actual being? You are talking all the time about something that is not Truth.*

You would have to remain established in the Native State of Being and Radiate from <u>That</u> in the form of life, to be <u>true</u>.

DANIEL: *This is What we have all been drawn to in You, Beloved Master. It is a fundamental reason why we all came here.*

AVATAR ADI DA SAMRAJ: *Tcha.*[*1] *You must become relaxed from your agitated, contracted identification with the body-mind and its play, and become capable of simply Standing in the Native Position. Then all that Radiates from that Position informs the body-mind, informs the life, and you do not lose Reality in order to be alive. So "thoughtless feeling" is a simple way of describing what is Realized—Self-Existing, Self-Radiant, Non-conditional. Everything is Divinely Self-Recognizable in Reality—no longer the lie, the invented life made by dissociation from the Native State, but everything seen in Truth in and As the Divine Self-Condition, unobstructed Light, unobstructed Consciousness, One with all, Transcending all, in a flash of no time whatsoever.*

To recover What <u>Is</u>, forgetting the separate "I", even for a moment, is more than a matter of following the thread of meaning in this dialogue. When one is Graced to sit at the Feet of a Master, one is stepped out of the world and entered into the sphere of the Master's Radiance, the "field" of his or her innate Transmission of the state of Realization. The Words of Adi Da Samraj, as all His devotees can confess, carry a potency that is vastly beyond the verbal meaning, a force that activates fundamental transformations in the being. This potency is not restricted to hearing Him speak. He invests Himself Spiritually in all of His Writing, also, and

---

* Notes to the Text of *The Perfect Tradition* appear on pp. 129–37.

that Transmission of His Person can be received through reading this book.

The Hidden Structure of the Body-Mind

The effort to console, or "save", or transform, or even dissolve the apparent "I"—which we all presume to be—is a major preoccupation of religion. In fact, as Adi Da Samraj argues, this search, in all its variant forms, is basically the entirety of religion. And He goes further, bringing the extraordinary insight that the kind of religion (or even rejection of religion) that one settles for depends on what dimension of the "I" one is focused in.

In the ancient oriental view, the "I" is more than the body, and more than merely "body and soul". Rather, the human being is a complex psycho-physical structure composed of a hierarchy of layers or sheaths.[2] In the simplest understanding, this esoteric anatomy is composed of three fundamental dimensions—which Adi Da Samraj defines as "gross, subtle, and causal", or "outer, inner, and root".

The gross (or outer) dimension corresponds to the physical level of experience and the waking state.

The subtle (or inner) dimension includes everything to do with mind, emotion, and energy—including the domain of dreaming and psychic experience, as well as the range of supernormal experience that is commonly called "mystical".

The causal (or root) dimension refers to the depth where the "I"-"other" sense originates, thereby "causing", or generating, the worlds of subtle and gross experience that extend from that root presumption of separate "identity".

As Adi Da Samraj makes clear in *Religion and Reality* (the second book in the "Perfect Knowledge" Series), popular, or exoteric, religion is strictly an outer, waking-state affair, motivated by the concerns of physical existence. Whatever its particular characteristics of doctrine and practice in any time and place, exoteric religion is a search for consolation and salvation through belief in some kind of "Creator-God" or patron-deity, and an adherence to a moral code of behavior that promotes social order.

The esoteric traditions, accounting for a small minority of humanity's religious endeavors, conduct a more refined and inward form of seeking. They aspire to transcend the common myths and Awaken directly to What is Ultimate. They all speak, in one way or another, of Realizing an Ultimate Source-Condition of the impermanent, arising world. But this intention has various meanings and implications, depending on the orientation of the particular tradition. In summary, there is not only a fundamental difference between the exoteric religions and the esoteric traditions, but real differences between the esoteric schools themselves.

Throughout His writings, Avatar Adi Da's revelation is that these differences correspond with the esoteric anatomy just described (with its gross, subtle, and causal dimensions). Esoteric practitioners are focused <u>either</u> in the subtle dimension, which is the realm of the various mystical and Yogic traditions, <u>or</u> in the causal dimension, which is the domain of the Sages, the Realizers who are exclusively invested in knowing the Transcendental Reality. Thus, the esoteric traditions of humankind have been polarized around these two different orientations—the orientation to subtle energy and light as the means and nature of Realization, on the one hand, and the urge to Realize Consciousness, independent of objects, on the other.

Of Avatar Adi Da's communications about Reality, one dimension that is of greatest use to our global human culture is what He has described as "the seven stages of life". These stages—described in detail on pp. 79–127 in this book—constitute a fully-developed "map" of the progressive developmental potential of the human being, based on its total structure—gross, subtle, and causal.

The various stages of life are illustrated not only in the individual case, but also in the cultural evidence of history. Adi Da Samraj refers to the vast and varied process of humanity's wisdom-search as the "Great Tradition", and explains how it can be understood in terms of six stages of life—with the potential for the Realization of the seventh (or most ultimate) stage of life. His paradigm of the progressive stages of life represents an esoteric science that is highly detailed and extremely precise.

In a conversation with His devotees, Adi Da Samraj speaks here of the great shift that must occur before the ordinary human being—still struggling to adapt in the foundation stages of psycho-physical development (the first three stages of life)—can take the leap into the fourth stage of life, characterized by a life of devotional communion with the Divine Spirit (however the Divine is conceived or experienced).

The first three stages of life are associated with the most basic physical, emotional, mental, and sexual functions to which you have adapted. The transition to the fourth stage of life requires a realistic confrontation with your limitations in the first three stages of life. You must go through the inevitable and natural crisis of this transition, and that is a profound matter. If it were not profound, most difficult, and something that people in general are not prepared for, human beings all over the world would have entered the fourth stage of life by now. This crisis of transition is the most profound and unwelcome change that confronts humanity. That change has been unwelcome for thousands of years.

—October 4, 1985

In terms of the underlying structure of the gross, subtle, and causal dimensions, the transition to the fourth stage of life is, as Adi Da Samraj indicates, the most critical transition, because it represents the first entry into the domain of that which is beyond the physical. The fourth stage of life is a bridge between the gross and the subtle. It involves an opening of the body-mind to the dimension of Spiritual Energy, which transforms the beliefs and observances of merely exoteric religion into a real heart-practice and potential mystical experience.

In the fifth stage of life the fundamental "point of view" is no longer that of the waking state, but, rather, a persistent concentration in the subtle-energy centers in and above the head, in order to enter into states of ascended bliss—possibly including the experience of subtle lights, visions, sounds, and tastes.

The sixth stage of life goes to the causal root. The effort of sixth stage practitioners is to abide as the Formless Reality (or Consciousness) that is intuited in the depth of meditative contemplation, and to discount (or turn away from) all experience (gross and subtle), in order to find and stay in touch with that Root-Reality.

The Final Esoteric Secret

Avatar Adi Da's discovery of the "seven stages" paradigm was not a product of merely philosophical enquiry but a tacit clarity that arose during His youthful quest to recover the "Bright". The tradition with which He was most directly associated during that time was that of Kundalini Yoga. His first Spiritual Master was Rudi (Swami Rudrananda), who worked in New York. Later, in India, Avatar Adi Da's Gurus included some of the greatest Siddhas, or Master-Yogis and Spiritual Transmitters, of modern times—including Swami Muktananda, Rang Avadhoot, and Swami Nityananda (then deceased). The principle of their teaching was the "Shakti"— the Spirit-Power transmitted from Master to devotee, which awakens the chakras (or esoteric energy-vortices in the spinal line) from base to crown.

While Adi Da Samraj freely experienced all the potential of Kundalini Yoga during His association with these Masters, He was never satisfied that the experiences and samadhis—no matter how dramatic or apparently profound—amounted to Ultimate Enlightenment. Throughout His youth, in fact, He experienced breakthroughs of the "Bright" that established Him in a "radical" disposition relative to all the traditional forms of esoteric practice. Thus, He brought a unique intelligence to whatever arose to His experience. After His Re-Awakening to the "Bright" in 1970,[3] the esoteric anatomy underpinning His entire Spiritual adventure was obvious to Him, and was eventually systematically described by Him in terms of seven stages of life.

One of the most remarkable aspects of Avatar Adi Da's account of His quest to recover the "Bright" is His description of a previously unknown Yogic process that leads from fixation in the chakra system (exemplifying the fifth stage of life) into the causal dimension (associated with the sixth stage of life), and then into the Ultimate Yogic Form that characterizes the seventh stage of life.

The following passages, selected from *The Knee Of Listening*, illustrate the developments in this process. The first passage—from Avatar Adi Da's recounting of His myriad experiences in the mode of Kundalini Yoga—describes a classic vision of the ascending process associated with the fifth stage of life. This vision occurred while Adi Da Samraj was on retreat in Swami Muktananda's company in Mumbai in 1969.

I saw the muladhar appear below me as a Siva-lingam.[4] Then I appeared below, my hands tied to the lingam in a gesture of prayer, pointing above. I rose up with the lingam into the sahasrar and experienced the perfect, Infinite, Unmoved Sat-Chit-Ananda—the Pure Existence-Consciousness-Bliss of the Indian Godhead, my own Ultimate Self-Nature as the Divine Being of all the world's scriptures.

The next passage describes an event in February 1970, when Adi Da was living a reclusive life in an apartment in New York:

For several nights, I was awakened again and again with sharp lateral pains in my head. They felt like deep incisions in my skull and brain, as if I were undergoing a surgical operation. During the day following the last of these experiences, I realized a marvelous relief. I saw that what appeared as the sahasrar (the terminal chakra and primary lotus in the crown of the head) had been severed. The sahasrar had fallen off like a blossom. The Shakti—Which had previously appeared as a polarized Energy that moved up and down through the various chakras (or functional centers), producing various effects—was now released from the chakra form. There was no more polarized Force. Indeed, there was no structure whatsoever—no up or down, no chakras. . . .

Previously, all the universes seemed built and dependent upon that foundation structure of descending and ascending Energy—such that the nature and value of any given experience was determined by the level of the chakra in which the humanly-born conscious awareness was functioning. . . . But now I saw that Reality (and Real Consciousness) was not in the least determined by any form apart from Itself. Consciousness had shown Its inherent Freedom and Priority in relation to the chakra form. It had shown Itself to be senior to that entire structure, Prior to every kind of manifestation or modification of cosmic Energy (or Shakti).

From the "point of view" of the stages of life, Adi Da Samraj was now passing through a process associated with the sixth stage of life. But the esoteric anatomy behind this profound spontaneous shift into the Consciousness dimension prior to Energy became fully clear to Him only after His Re-Awakening to the "Bright" seven months later (in

September, 1970). Soon after that great Event (described in detail in *The Knee Of Listening*), He wrote:

I realized that, in the context of natural appearances, I am Communicated through a specific center in the body. Relative to the body, I appear to reside in the heart—but to the right side of the chest. I press upon a point approximately two inches to the right of the center of the chest. This is the seat of Reality and Real Consciousness.

Around this time, Adi Da Samraj began to recollect, and further investigate, sayings of Ramana Maharshi in which Ramana Maharshi indicates that the doorway to the Transcendental Self in the human being is located at a psycho-physical locus in the right side of the chest. The traditions of Transcendental Realization (notably Advaita Vedanta and classical Buddhism) do not, in general, associate Realization with any psycho-physical locus—perhaps because the entire effort of the sixth-stage Realizer is to ignore psycho-physical experience and to dwell in the "cave" of Consciousness alone. Thus, the association between the causal dimension and the right side of the heart has scarcely been acknowledged in the Great Tradition.

In January 1971, in Los Angeles, the nature of Avatar Adi Da's unique Yogic process was fully clarified. He had a revelatory experience of the "design" (or form) of the "Bright" as It manifests in the context of the body-mind. He later identified this form as the "Amrita Nadi", or "nerve of immortal bliss", alluded to in a few traditional sources (including remarks of Ramana Maharshi), but without any evidence of an experiential awareness of its real structure. Adi Da Samraj writes in *The Knee Of Listening*:

That morning (as I sat in meditation with two of my devotees), my body suddenly jolted and twisted strongly on its spinal axis as the "Bright" Divine Spirit-Current moved up

*from my heart, via the right side, to the crown of my head,
and above—even into the most ascended Matrix of the
"Bright" Divine Spirit-Power, infinitely above the body and the
cosmic domain. In the instant of that ascent, there was a loud
cracking sound (also heard by the others in the room), as if
my neck had been broken. And, in that instant in which the
Amrita Nadi showed Its "regenerated" Form in me, I (as had
no one else before me) directly observed Its Shape. It is an
S-Shaped Form, beginning in the right side of the heart (but
including the entire heart region), then ascending in a curve
along the front side of the upper chest, then passing back-
wards (through the throat), then curving upwards again (but
via the back of the skull), finally curving toward the crown of
the head (and, from thence, to the Matrix of Light infinitely
above the crown of the head). Therefore, it is this Ultimate (or
truly "regenerated") Form (or Most Ultimate Realization)
of the Amrita Nadi—this "regenerated" Circuit and Current of
Spiritual Love-Bliss, Which passes in an S-Shaped double-
curve, front to back, from the heart (on the right side) to the
crown of the head and to the Matrix of Light infinitely above
the crown of the head—that I declare to be the perfect Form,
the Form of Truth, the Form of Reality, the Form of the Heart.
I call that "regenerated" Form (experienced in the living context of the total body-mind) "the 'Bright'". Even from birth, I
have Known the "Bright". It has, ever since my birth, been the
guiding and revealing foundation of my life. And the "Bright"
(in Its Totality) is the most ultimate Realization and revelation
of my "Brightly"-born life.*

No "Argument" Between Consciousness and Energy

The regeneration of this Ultimate Yogic Form in the case of
Adi Da Samraj is momentous beyond comprehension. What
His Realization reveals is the unique structure that resolves
what one could call the traditional esoteric "argument"

between the "Consciousness point of view" and the "Energy point of view". The Sages, drawn to the causal root, declare the pristine depth of Consciousness to be the only Truth. The Yogic practitioners, turned up toward the sahasrar, regard the psycho-physics of Energy to be the means of Realization. But the potential of a connection between the right side of the heart and the sahasrar has never been comprehended or Realized. That connection is potential in the fully Awakened Amrita Nadi—the living Current that inherently Stands between the right side of the heart and the Matrix of Light Above. This Realization is beyond both the fifth stage of life and the sixth stage of life. Amrita Nadi is the esoteric structure of a further stage of life—the seventh stage of life, a Realization that has never before been described. In the seventh stage of life, Reality is Self-Revealed as both Consciousness and Energy, or Conscious Light—the "Bright". And that Realization is Non-conditional, requiring no effort or intention to maintain. In the words of Adi Da Samraj, it is "Open Eyes"—the "Perfect Knowledge" of Reality.

Such is the Realization of the Avataric Great Sage, Adi Da Samraj, and such is the nature of His Spiritual Transmission. Therefore, ordinary human beings related to Him as devotees have, at times, by His Grace, experienced this incomparably profound Revelation of the structure of Reality—not yet as a permanent Realization, but as deep glimpses that motivate the being to the great ordeal that perfect Realization requires. One such profound occasion, which took place in 1988, is described in the following account.

Adi Da Samraj had been gathered with devotees for many hours, engaged in Discourse and dialogue. Then, as was His wont at that time, He would dance—either alone or with devotees. This was not ordinary dancing by any stretch of the imagination. It was always a Divine Revelation and

Instruction to whomever He was engaging in the dance, and to everyone in the room. As Adi Da Samraj said at the end of one of these evenings, "When I dance, I move through all possible planes before I finish. I dance to not to have to dance again."

On the occasion described here, someone had put on a recording of a devotee chanting the *Ruchira Avatara Gita*, which is Avatar Adi Da's own rendering of the traditional *Guru Gita*.

JULIE ANDERSON: At the end of the night, Beloved Adi Da stood to Dance the chant, Ruchira Avatara Gita. *His body was literally swollen with Love and His skin took on a hue of brilliant blue and reddish tones, "Bright" and also seemingly bruised with the tender Fullness of His Love-Blissful Being. The Radiance emanating from His body filled the room with a lustrous mist of white light, and His Presence was so thick in the room, you could literally breathe Him in. Every Movement Radiated His Blessing out in waves as He, literally and by Dance, extended His Love in all directions from every portion of His Divine Body.*

My whole being rushed toward Him, in a feeling of Spiritual embrace—falling into a deep rest in His Spiritual Presence. My visual perception of everything around me dissolved in His Blissful and pervasive Light, until there was only His Dancing Form. I was being absorbed into His Love-Bliss— there was absolutely no resistance, no effort, no thought.

As I was most willingly and helplessly Drawn into sublime union with Him, I began to notice that there was no boundary of the body-mind left. I could no longer differentiate between what was internal and what was external. There was no separation, no sense of separate self, no sense of "other"—only Fullness, without obstruction.

I began to notice that His Spiritual-Current had reached a point of such Sublimity that It became Moveless. As that

Feeling persisted, all sense of the body-mind dissolved. Only an awareness of a pinpoint (or locus), a matrix of extremely "Bright" Light radiating down from above, and a point (or location), deep in the heart on the right side remained.

Then, there was a driving Force piercing the right side of the heart and pressing through to a Place of Perfection that is indescribable. Everything dissolved in This. I now had no awareness of any perception, internal or external—no sense of anything except for this absolute Feeling of Him, the Love-Bliss-Fullness of His Being.

There was not even "one" or "I" left to feel this. There was only the conscious, utterly self-less enjoyment of His Non-conditional State of Love-Bliss.

He had Gifted me with the direct Glimpse of His State in this experience.

The "Radical" Understanding of the Ego

Various Eastern traditions have emphasized the "Non-dual" nature of Truth and Reality. Much has been said about non-dualism—but to actually go beyond dualism in real practice, rather than as mere philosophy, is a great matter. It means transcending the dual structure of conventional awareness—the sense of "self" and "other", or the "I" over against everything else—in a process that can be called "ego-death". Oriental culture, on the whole, takes a negative view of the body and of physical (or gross) existence. Thus, there is a tendency to dissociate from conditions and to idealize the ascetical life as a way to minimize or eliminate the ego and "get to" What is Beyond. But, as Adi Da Samraj has always pointed out, asceticism—in and of itself—does not lead to true "ego-death", because it is, ultimately, an attempt by the ego to eliminate the ego! To really transcend the ego-"I", which is the most fundamental structure in consciousness, requires a more "radical" approach.

On April 25, 1972, the evening that He began His formal Teaching-Work, Adi Da Samraj expounded His own "radical" understanding of what the ego-"I" is, as opposed to the traditional understanding.

Ramana Maharshi advised seekers to find out <u>who</u> it is that asks the question, thinks the thought, and so on. But that "who" is, in Reality, not an "entity". When Ramana Maharshi spoke, He used the symbolic language of Advaita Vedanta. . . . The imagery of this traditional description of the process of Realizing Truth deals in statics, "things"-in-space. Therefore, in that traditional description, there is <u>the</u> ego—the objectified, solidified self.

But I speak in terms of process, or movement. I speak in terms of concepts of experience with which the modern mind is more familiar—and which more accurately reflect the actual nature of conditionally manifested reality. Thus, I do not speak of the ego as an "object" within a conceptual universe of objects. The concept of the "static ego" is no longer very useful—and, indeed, it is false and misleading.

Therefore, what has traditionally been called "the ego" is rightly understood to be an activity. And "radical" self-understanding is that direct seeing of the fundamental (and always present) activity that is suffering, ignorance, distraction, motivation, and dilemma. When that activity is most perfectly understood, then there is Spontaneous and Nonconditional Realization of That Which had previously been excluded from conscious awareness—That Which Is Always Already the Case.

—*My "Bright" Word*, p. 82

The ego-activity, as Adi Da Samraj explained that night—and has continued to emphasize ever since—is self-contraction, a recoil in conscious awareness. From this ego-act stem all our notions about reality. We see an apparent world of separate beings and things from a point of awareness that we call "I". This is the world we presume to live in, the world we think is real. But it is real only from a limited "point of view". And it is not a "free" world. It is a world fraught with the bondage of frenetic seeking—the never-ending search to overcome the core ego-stress that is our fundamental (and self-created) suffering.

Such is the root not only of the searches of ordinary life, but of the religious and Spiritual quest as well. In the words of Adi Da Samraj, there are, in fact, "three egos", or the same activity of self-contraction operating at each level of the human mechanism—gross, subtle, and causal. The ego-search at the gross level is the wandering in all the possibilities of the waking body-mind. The same search at the subtle level is the pursuit of mystical experience and "Spiritual" goals. The causal level of the search is the effort to get beyond all experience and all sense of "I" through one or another technique.

During His junior year at Columbia College, Adi Da Samraj had a sudden, profound experience that revealed to Him this depth structure of self-contraction and the Condition that is Prior to it. The context for this experience was a bold experiment that Adi Da Samraj had been engaging for the previous two years. Out of utter despair at finding Truth in any traditional source, and certainly not in the university ethos in which He was living, He had chosen an extreme course. On the streets of New York and in every kind of circumstance, He had abandoned Himself to the gamut of experience, unrestrained by social taboos, in the hope that Truth, or God, or Reality would be revealed through the intensity of His search. He writes in *The Knee Of Listening*:

On this extraordinary night, I sat at my desk late into the night. I had exhausted my seeking, such that I felt there were no more books to read, no possible kinds of ordinary experience *that could exceed what I had already embraced. There seemed no outstanding sources for any new excursion, no remaining and conclusive possibilities. I was drawn into the interior tension of my mind that held all of that seeking—every impulse and alternative, every motive in the form of my desiring. I contemplated it as a whole, a dramatic singleness, and it moved me into a profound shape of life-feeling, such that all the vital centers in my body and mind appeared like a long funnel of contracted planes that led on to an infinitely regressed and invisible image. I observed this deep sensation of conflict and endlessly multiplied contradictions, such that I was surrendered to its very shape, as if to experience it perfectly and to <u>be</u> it.*

Then, quite suddenly, in a moment, I experienced a total revolution in my body-mind, and (altogether) in my humanly-born conscious awareness. An absolute sense of understanding opened and arose at the extreme end of all this sudden contemplation. And all of the motions of me that moved down into that depth appeared to reverse their direction at some unfathomable point. The rising impulse caused me to stand, and I felt a surge of Force draw up out of my depths and expand, Filling my entire body and every level of my humanly-born conscious awareness with wave on wave of the most Beautiful and Joyous Energy.

I felt absolutely mad, but the madness was not of a desperate kind. There was no seeking and no dilemma within it, no question—no unfulfilled motive, not a single object or presence outside myself.

I could not contain the Energy in my small room. I ran out of the building and through the streets. I thought, if I could only find someone to talk to, to communicate to about this "Thing". The Energy in my body was overwhelming, and there was an ecstasy in every cell that was almost intolerable in its Pressure, Light, and Force.

It took me many years to understand that revolution in my living being. . . . It marked the rising in me of fundamental and

Non-conditional Life, and it, in its moment, removed every shadow of dilemma and ignorance from the mind, on every level, and all its effects in the body.

While the experience itself passed, a knowledge arose from it, which Adi Da Samraj calls "radical" understanding:

> *I saw that the Truth or Reality was a matter of the absence of all contradictions, of every trace of conflict, opposition, division, or desperate motivation within. Where there is no seeking, no contradiction, there is only the Non-conditional Knowledge and Power that is Reality. This was the first aspect of that sudden Clarity.*
>
> *In this State beyond all contradiction, I also saw that Freedom and Joy is not attained, that It is not dependent on any form, object, idea, progress, or experience.*
>
> —*The Knee Of Listening*

The Columbia experience took place in 1960, when Adi Da Samraj was only twenty years old. And so, even before He approached His Gurus, He had understood the ego as self-contraction, and seen the worlds of seeking that it generates. He had made the "radical" discovery that the very search for Truth is the obstruction to Realizing Truth, because seeking is always based on the presumption and activity of separation from That Which Exists.

Thus, Avatar Adi Da's time with His Gurus was not, as in the usual case, for the purpose of Realizing the Truth, but for the purpose of learning what esoteric Masters have believed to be the Truth, and how they have attempted to get there. All the while, "radical" self-understanding was His steady foundation, until the Realization that was coincident with His Birth emerged again in its fullness.

As Adi Da Samraj has always Taught, human beings in the general case simply want to fulfill their ego-search, at whatever level of reality they are focused—gross, subtle, or causal. The disposition of "radical" understanding is to transcend the root "clench" in consciousness that is generating the search at every level.

Adi Da Samraj sometimes refers to the first six stages of life as the "psycho-biography" of the ego, because these stages represent all the potential that the apparent persona can experience or achieve, by "playing" its structural mechanism—gross, subtle, and causal. In the midst of that vast range of possibility, however, the fundamental ego-activity, the motivated search, remains the same. At the causal depth, all that is left is the root-ego, the barest sense of separateness, just the awareness of "I" and "other", and the effort to resolve that last duality. That is the place where the greatest Sages have, to one or another degree, "leaped off" the edge into the non-dual Knowledge of the Transcendental Self, or the Nirvanic Truth.

That is the place to which the youthful Adi Da Samraj would spontaneously return in His periodic revery of contemplating the great stone. He knew intuitively that the Truth lay in understanding the mysterious coincidence between the Transcendental Reality and the apparent world. But none of His experiences, none of His Teachers, could explain this. The Answer came, in the end, through the force of His own "radical" self-understanding—which enabled Him to transcend all the partial messages of Truth delivered through the psycho-physics of the body-mind and Re-Awaken to the "Bright", the Inherently egoless Condition, beyond all seeking and all "difference".

The Perfect Tradition

In 1980, two devotees of Adi Da Samraj visited Chogyam Trungpa (a well-known Tibetan teacher, then working in America). They showed him video footage of Adi Da Samraj sitting in silent Darshan and speaking to devotees. After receiving the presentation, Chogyam Trungpa expressed his respect for the authenticity of Adi Da Samraj, and made the comment: "It is tremendously difficult to begin a new tradition."

In fact, when Adi Da Samraj began to Teach, it was not His intention to found a new tradition. In 1973, Avatar Adi Da even requested a formal interview with Swami Muktananda to determine whether He could establish His own Ashram and impart His Revelation of the "Bright" in association with, and continuous with, the Siddha-Lineage represented by Swami Nityananda and Swami Muktananda. He was already acknowledged by Swami Muktananda as a formal sannyasin within that Lineage.

But this was not to be. And, so, Adi Da Samraj was without a means of linking Himself to any existing school within the Great Tradition. Thus, He began to develop His Spiritual Work as a new and independent tradition—with all the sacred, cooperative, creative, organizational, cultural, and dharmic dimensions that such a profound undertaking requires. A religious tradition is not merely a teaching and a series of practices, but a way of life that covers all modes of experience and aspiration. It is the highest cultural endeavor, which ordinarily develops organically over a very long period of time. The practices of the fifth and sixth stage type that have taken root in the West have not originated there. They have come out of the ancient Eastern cultures, transported and transmuted into a Western context by the efforts of individual teachers and the publication of traditional texts.

Thus, there is no precedent for the effort that Adi Da Samraj is making to establish, in His lifetime, the Way of "Perfect Knowledge" (or Way of Adidam) as a new tradition—a total culture of life and practice that includes and serves the process of Realization from the beginner's level to the ultimate stages, or "Perfect Practice", of the Way. At the same time, His Way of "Perfect Knowledge", does not, as He says here, appear "in a vacuum":

There is an authoritative source-tradition within the Great Tradition, with which the Way of Adidam is continuous, and which, therefore, provides a basis for understanding the Way of Adidam. The uniqueness of the Way I have Revealed and Given does not exist in a vacuum. The Way of Adidam is, ultimately, the Perfect Tradition, but there is a dimension at the heights of all the Transcendentalist (or sixth stage) schools within the Great Tradition that is compatible with It—simply lacking the final step, which is the seventh stage of life.

The previous modes of Perfect Teaching—exemplified in the traditions of Advaita Vedanta and Buddhism[5]—were not Perfect in the most ultimate sense that I describe as the seventh stage of life. They were Perfect in the secondary, or preliminary, sense. They were precursors—but they did not achieve the Most Perfect Realization, and they do not carry the Most Perfect Revelation and Teaching. The sixth stage teachings are based in the causal dimension, which means they are yet psycho-physically based. This does not at all mean that they are to be ignored, but simply makes it plain where their views come from, and how, ultimately, the seventh stage Realization goes beyond all of that.

The Way of Adidam that I have Revealed and Given covers all the stages of life. It is not just a Transcendentalist Way. It covers the entire process of human possibility and Realization from the beginning—everything gross, everything subtle, everything of a causal nature. And these dimensions are not merely exploited for the sake of developing those possibilities, but "covered" in the sense that you must go beyond them, and there are disciplines that relate to all the potential kinds of experience.

Thus, the Way of Adidam exists with reference to the Great Tradition, but it is a universal Teaching, not an Eastern teaching.

—April 21, 2005 and March 3, 2006

In order to indicate that the Way of Adidam is continuous with Advaita Vedanta and Buddhism, and the actual completion of these traditions (and the entire Great Tradition), Adi Da Samraj has given alternative names to His Way of "Perfect Knowledge" that indicate this connection and continuity—including "Advaitayana Buddhism", and "Buddhayana Advaitism" (p. 92).

The Way of Adidam combines and transcends the two different orientations represented by Buddhism and Advaita Vedanta—the emphasis (in Buddhism) on discriminating what is merely conditional, or "not-self", and the emphasis (in Advaita Vedanta) on directly identifying with the Absolute Reality, or Transcendental Self. From the beginning, Adi Da Samraj has called His devotees to find their impulse to ego-transcendence based on a "dual sensitivity"—a sensitivity to what is merely conditional and passing, on the one hand, and to What is Non-Conditional, Transcendental and Divine, on the other.

The means of this dual sensitivity is not "mindfulness" (in the Buddhist sense) or a discriminative effort to locate the Ultimate Reality beyond objects (in the Advaitic sense). The Means of practice and of Realization in the Way of Adidam is Adi Da Samraj Himself and His direct Transmission of the "Bright", the Conscious Light That Is Reality.

In the Way of Adidam, the devotional relationship to Adi Da Samraj is the circumstance in which He Grants His great Transmission of the "Bright". As He has frequently pointed out, it is not possible to simply "work towards" the Most Perfect Knowledge of Reality, or, otherwise, to merely declare It to be so. That Knowledge must be Given, directly Transmitted, from the Source. Avatar Adi Da is always Radiating His Inherently "Bright" Condition—but, before His devotee can become fully available to His Spiritual Transmission, "radical" self-understanding must unlock the self-contracted body-mind, and let Him in. This most fundamental capability to transcend egoity, moment to moment, is also a Gift of His Grace that awakens on the basis of profound preparation.

Devotional heart-Communion with the Avataric Great Sage, Adi Da Samraj, <u>and</u> the observation, understanding, and transcending of self-contraction are the two pillars of the Way of "Perfect Knowledge" He has Given. This is true from the beginning—until, in the Awakening to the seventh stage of life, the ego is most perfectly understood. Even so, devotion to Avatar Adi Da does not cease. Rather, devotion to Him is perfected in the seventh stage of life, through utter identification with His Spiritually "Bright" Divine State. All the various disciplines and practices that Adi Da Samraj gives to purify and bring equanimity to the body-mind are merely supportive to these two great pillars of the Way, and never techniques or methods to be applied independently.

The miracle of the Way of Adidam—and a primary reason it is rightly described as the "Perfect Tradition"—is that the Transmission and intuition of the seventh stage of life is given from the beginning. Potentially, in any occasion of His Darshan—but particularly in the moments when He Sits silently with devotees—Adi Da Samraj simply, directly, and profoundly Reveals the Root-Realization that the entire Way of "Perfect Knowledge" is about. The mere beholding of Him in quiet, heart-open attentiveness dissolves the edges and opacity of the physical world. An inherent underlying Radiance permeates the view, and everything, including His apparent human Form, Reveals Itself as a fluid Light of infinite Blissful depth. There is a deep relaxation of the knot of "I", a kind of amazement at the obvious illusion of separateness by which the ordinary life is motivated. Nothing at all has happened, and yet, Reality is Self-Manifest and the true nature of the arising world has become obvious. It is literally nothing more than an unnecessary and harmless mirage rising and falling in the timeless Ocean of Reality. And Adi Da Samraj is That One. He is the Source and the Nature of What Is, Gracefully Appearing through the Agency of a human Form. All of this is shown to be simply so, and the heart breaks at the Wonder of It, and the Love of It, and the sheer sudden Truth of It. The numinous Stone that was contemplated by Adi Da Samraj in His youth has become, for His devotees, the All-Revealing Mystery of His own human Form.

Avatar Adi Da's Transmission of Reality is the Source of His Way of "Perfect Knowledge", and therefore of its Perfection. Ultimately, the Way of Adidam is a Divine Yoga of "Brightening" that exceeds all precedent and human comprehension. And yet, it is entirely real. Every detail of it has been Revealed by Adi Da Samraj not only in His Words, but in the most profound bodily and Spiritual ordeal and Sublime Signs, which His devotees have witnessed and continue to observe every day. He is showing, in a manner that surpasses all the myths, what was anciently meant by the term "Avatar"—the Descent into human Form of That Which Is Beyond—the Transcendental, Divine Condition made visible and alive to human eyes.

The Urgency of Truth

In the tradition of the *Bhagavad Gita,* the appearance of an Avatar coincides with degenerate times and an overwhelming human need for Divine Intervention.

> *Whenever a decrease of righteousness exists,*
> *And there is a rising up of unrighteousness,*
> *Then I give forth myself*
> *For the protection of the good. . . .*
> *For the sake of establishing righteousness,*
> *I come into being from age to age.*[6]

Few serious people would disagree that we are now living in such a time. The great Wisdom-Teachings of the past have ceased to be the living Truth for human beings. Rather, a very superficial sense of Reality has replaced the natural participatory awareness of the nature of existence. It is said that a little knowledge is a dangerous thing—and that is the present plight of humanity. For all its cleverness, the modern Homo sapiens is not sapient enough. We know enough about the laws of physics and biology to exploit— and potentially destroy—our planet, and yet we remain largely ignorant of What Is, beyond our sensory and mental experience.

The Avataric Great Sage, Adi Da Samraj, is profoundly concerned about where contemporary human culture is going. As He has always pointed out, the modern world has settled for a very narrow slice of the total spectrum of human understanding.

Adi Da's Message, in all of His writings, is that there is only one force in human affairs that can correct the terrible trajectory of the world today. The "decline and fall" of global civilization is inevitable, unless a greater knowledge of Reality can begin to affect human culture. Locating this greater knowledge, and bringing it to bear in real human life, both individual and collective, is the most critical issue for all humankind. To convey the urgency of Truth, the Truth about Reality, is the incomparably creative lifetime-effort of Avatar Adi Da Samraj. His offering of the books in the "Perfect Knowledge" Series is part of that Work. In these extraordinary, all-encompassing books, He explains the Great Tradition to itself, illumines its hidden treasures, and Reveals the Perfect Tradition that resolves the great wisdom-search in a Place never fully found before. ■

I <u>Am</u> The Avataric Divine Gift of The "Bright"— and of The "Thumbs" That Reveals It

The Avataric Divine Self-Revelation of Adi Da Samraj

I.

From the beginning of My here-Born Life, I have Known a perfect Alternative to the oppressive internal dilemma of My natural existence. I have played in the problem of My alternatives, but, from My earliest experience of life, I have Enjoyed a Condition that, as an infant child, I Named and Called the "Bright".

I have always known desire, not merely for extreme pleasures of the senses and the mind, but for the highest Enjoyment of Spiritual Energy and Capability. But I have not been seated in desire, and desire has only been a play that I have grown to understand, and to enjoy without conflict, and to transcend—within the Sphere of My Inherent Finality. I have always been Seated in the "Bright".

Even as a baby, I remember only crawling around, inquisitively, with a boundless Feeling of Joy, Light, and Freedom in the middle of My head. My head-to-toe was Bathed in Energy, Moving Unobstructed, in a Circle—down from Above, all the way down, then Up, all the way Up, and around again—and always, first and most, Shining from My heart. It was an Expanding Sphere of Joy from the heart. And I was a Radiant Form—the Source of Energy, Love-Bliss, and Light in the midst of a world that is entirely Energy, Love-Bliss, and Light. I was the Power of Reality Itself. I was a direct Enjoyment and Communication of the One Reality. I was the Heart Itself, Who Lightens the mind and all things. I was the same as every one and every thing—except, it became clear that others were apparently unaware of the "Thing" Itself.

Even as a little child, I Recognized It and Knew It, and My life was not a matter of anything else. That Awareness, That Conscious Enjoyment, That Self-Existing and Self-Radiant Space of Infinitely and Inherently Free Being, That Indivisible Shine of Inherent Joy, Standing in the heart, and

Expanding Freely from the heart, to All-Above, and, then, to all-below, Is the "Bright". As a little infant child, I spontaneously Named It the "Bright". And It Is the entire and Illimitable Source of My Always and Unquenchable True Humor. It Is Reality Itself. It is not separate from anything.

From My Birth, I have not been centered in the dilemma of My natural alternatives—but I have been entirely "Located" in and <u>As</u> the "Bright" Itself. So, it is with True Humor that I Describe how I existed all this time.

The Reason for My Birth was a spontaneous Motivation associated with a painful Loving of the people around Me. It was not merely compassion for them, as if they were poor people I could help. It was a painful emotional and physical Sensation in My heart, and in My solar plexus. It was profoundly painful, even then, and it always has been. It was associated with the full knowledge that the people to whom I was committing Myself were going to <u>die</u>—and that <u>I</u> would die, too. I knew that, if I agreed to be Incarnated in this natural life-form and circumstance—if I <u>became</u> this body and its lifetime—I would also die its death. And I knew that, as this bodily incarnate being, I was, in due course, going to be separated from every one and every thing I loved in its lifetime.

This was all fully obvious to Me—and, yet, this spontaneous Gesture, this painful Loving, this profound Sensation, Awakened to Awake in Me, and It Moved Me into the body, and It, altogether, Animated Me physically. Thus, it was, altogether and simply, a sympathetic Response that Brought Me into the sphere of human conditions, and of gross conditions altogether. That Response was identification with mortal existence—but it took place by Means of Delight. In My Inherent "Bright" Exaltation, even the wound of mortality was Forgotten. Thus, it was not the noticing of mortality, in and of itself, that generated My Movement into this plane. Rather, it was the Love-Response, the attracted Response, in

Which all of the negative aspects of gross conditional existence were effectively forgotten—in Love, in Delight, in Love-Bliss, in My Inherent Heart-"Brightness".

In time, after My Own "Bright" Strength of Being had been (temporarily) undermined by My experience of the human world of conflict, illusion, and death, I began to see there was a fundamental difference, or a very basic unlikeness, between Myself and others—not a difference of ultimate essence, and not at all a social or (otherwise) merely physical difference, but a difference of "point of view", and of experience, and of life-practice. The "difference" was the "Bright"—the, to Me Alone, Self-Evident Obviousness of the "Bright".

Eventually, having been too much "schooled" by conventional religion, and, otherwise, being innately puzzled by the conventional mind and the disturbed manner of others, I (gradually, and only tentatively) accepted the three root-conventions of the common mind: the idea of "God" (as "Creator", and as separate from all "creation"), the idea of separate self (in My Case, and in all cases), and the idea of the world (as itself separate, and as itself composed of separate "things", or absolute and inherent differences).

My earliest childhood, from birth, and not merely some later, or more adult, time, was the period of My first Knowledge and Unfoldment of the "Bright"—Which I Intrinsically Knew to Be the Inherently Perfect Form of Reality Itself and the Source-Condition of all the conditions of life.

And What Is That—exactly?

It Is Consciousness Itself, Inherently Self-Radiant and Self-Awake. It Is the Real Condition of My simple human state. It Is the Ultimate Nature of My Native State—Prior to even any and all conditional experience. It has never appeared as strange or awesome, to Me. There Is no shadow—nothing hidden in It. It Is not motivated to act, or

to seek any goal of action at all. There Is—to It—no "else-
where", no "outside", no "Other". It has no sense of time.
Nor does It ever even begin to feel any kind of confusion,
or any identification with existence as separated personality
and problematic experience. It Is the Center of the life-
functions—but without dilemma or unconsciousness. There
Are no divisions in It. Radiant Spiritual Energy Is Inherently
Self-Communicated within It, and, Thus and Thereby, in and
via the entire body-mind. There Is Inherent Joy in the body,
a Luminous cell-life, a constant Respiration and Circulation
of Love-Bliss-Energy—and of Unlimited, Boundless Inherent
Pleasure. There Is a Spiritual Current of Energy in the heart,
That Rises into the head, via the throat. And That Same
Spiritual Current of Energy Is also Evident below the heart—
Rising Up into the heart from below. There Is a Circle
of Spiritual Energy, Surrounding and Circulating, in and
around the all of body-mind. That Circle Is Spaceless and
Boundless—but Its always Formless Matrix Is always Above
the head, and always Above the mind. And all of This
Moving Energy Originates As a Single Spiritual Source-
Current of Light and Life in the heart—and That Current Is,
by virtue of heart-Radiation Alone, Reflected and Felt at a
Pervasive Center Above, and deep within, the head. There Is
a constant Self-Radiation within this totality of entire Form,
including all of the body, and the Inherently Silent
Mindlessness That would otherwise erupt as all of mind. It
Is Intrinsic Joy in the heart, Reflected Above As heart-born
Enjoyment, constantly Received Above, and within the head.
And That Formless, Spaceless Form of Consciousness Is Self-
"Bright", Silent, and Full—Knowing Only and Entirely this
Divine Self-Condition, This Indivisible Reality, and seeing no
problem, no separation, in the fact of life.

This "Bright", This Real and Self-Existing and Self-Radiant
Consciousness, This Indivisible Conscious Light, Is the Perfect
Intrinsic Form of Reality Itself, and the Source-Condition of

the living condition of conditionally apparent everything. And It is never undone. It Is now. It Is Me. And It Is you— Prior to and Always Already Beyond your ego-"I" of body-mind. Now and always, every living being is arising within and Indivisibly As This Perfect "Bright" Form—Which Is the Perfect Intrinsic and Always Prior Form of life.

The "problem" is only that life is not lived As Real and Self-"Bright" Consciousness Itself. Instead, the One, and Inherently Indivisible, and Perfectly Non-conditional, and Self-Evidently Divine Conscious Light is confused with conditional and seemingly individuated experience—the mere fragments of Primal Energy reflected in the event of the human personality, and in the functions that operate by laws subconscious and unconscious to the human-born individual, or, otherwise, reflected in the waves of stranded Primal Energy that fascinate the body-mind in the superconscious patterns Above. When such confusions of false and egoic identity overwhelm and distract the heart into some division of the living structure of conditionally apparent existence, the heart is moved to great seeking in all the paired alternatives of life. Every course that is not simply the demonstration of Intrinsically Self-Evident "Bright" Consciousness Itself—direct, and Always Already Present—is a schism in one's living form.

Even all the eventual excursions of My Life beyond childhood showed this all the more to Me.

When I was an infant, and, then, a little boy, the "Bright" was My constant Knowledge of Reality. But the more tentative I became about the Intrinsic "Bright" Self-Reality, the more I felt Myself to be separate from Reality Itself—and also separated from even all that seems conditionally too, in the seeming-time of human things. In that manner, I became one who "listens" to Reality, as if It is a seeming "Other". And, over time, I even became one who seeks Reality, as if It were not yet Present. And the more I became a "listener", and then a seeker, the more the Intrinsic and Inherently "Perfect Knowledge" of Reality Itself became a <u>sometimes</u> Occasion, an overwhelming <u>sometimes</u> Event—a merely temporary "Enlightenment Experience" in time.

Therefore, the "Fault" <u>I</u> Chose to Happen in the "Bright" required yet My Ordeal of Life—Beyond the childhood door and house.

II.

From My early childhood, at apparently random times (usually as I either approached sleep or awoke from sleep—and, most dramatically, during seizures of childhood illness, as I would pass into delirium), I had an experience that felt like a mass of gigantic thumbs coming down from above, pressing into My throat (causing something of a gagging, and somewhat suffocating, sensation), and then pressing further (and, it seemed, would have expanded without limitation or end), into some form of Myself that was much larger than My physical body.

The "Thumbs"—which is the word I spontaneously made, as an infant child, to Name this frequently re-occurring experience—was not visible in the ordinary sense. I did not <u>see</u> the "Thumbs" then, or at anytime since. The "Thumbs" was not—and is not—visible to Me with My physical eyes, nor do I ever "hallucinate" the "Thumbs" pictorially. Yet, I have always very consciously <u>felt</u> the "Thumbs" as having a peculiar form and mobility—just as I (likewise) consciously Experience My Own otherwise invisible and greater Self-"Bright" Energy-Form.

Whenever the Experience of the "Thumbs" has "Happened", It immediately and completely Enters the totality of My living human form—and, also, the Totality of My otherwise invisible and greater Self-"Bright" Energy-Form.

The "Thumbs" has always appeared to Me like "tongues"— or the Arrow of an Overwhelmingly Descending Force— Coming down upon Me from Above, and down via My head and throat. And, when the "Thumbs" Thus Enters deep into My body, the electro-magnetic or otherwise energic balances of My living being are suddenly reversed. On several of the earliest remembered occasions, I felt as if the body had risen above the ground somewhat. And, thus, I was actually <u>levitated</u>—to one or another degree.

During the Event of the "Thumbs", the body always ceases to be polarized toward the ground, or to be oriented in the gravitational direction of the earth's center. There is always a strong reversal of polarity, communicated along a line of Force analogous to the spine. The physical body—as well as a clearly felt and completely discerned bodily-enveloping Energy-Form, that can be interiorly felt as analogous to, but detached from, the physical body—is felt to turn in a curve along the spine, and, then, forward, in the direction of the heart. And, when this reversal of Energy has taken place completely, I Reside in a totally different "Body"—Which also Contains, and even Supersedes, the physical body. That "Body" is <u>spherical</u> in shape. And the sensation of dwelling as that Energy-Form is completely peaceful. The physical body is completely relaxed, and polarized to the shape of this other (spherical) "Body". The mind becomes quieted—and, then, there is a movement in the field of awareness that goes even deeper, into a profound State of Self-Radiant Self-Consciousness—That <u>Is</u> beyond all that is merely physical, and That <u>Is</u> entirely free of thought and mind and ego-sense.

During the "Thumbs", I have always been easily able to relax to a Perfect Depth. And, then, the Energy moves to the base of the spine, and travels upwards along the spine, to the head. As the Energy does so, I feel the polarity of My physical being reverse—and, instead of tending gravitationally downward toward My seat, I "gravitate" Upwards, toward My head. As I relax completely, the reversal of Energy becomes complete—and My actual (or Self-Evident) Form feels to be a kind of detached sphere, entirely free of the ordinary body-sense. A tremendous sense of Peace and Fullness has always arisen at such times, and I, then, expect to remain in that State. But, I discovered early on, as soon as I would become attached to It, It would tend to disappear. So, then, I relax more. And, as I relax, an extraordinary depth appears within My humanly-born conscious aware-ness, and there is the feeling-sensation of falling into an Infinite Deep. Then, I always pass into a Profound and Shapeless Bliss.

From My earliest childhood time, after a cycle of the "Thumbs" would become complete, I would get up from the bed—or the chair, or whatever the body-situation of the moment of the Event. And I would, then, walk around, and beam Joyfully at the room. In every such Event, the Love-Blissful, unthreatened Current of the "Bright" Emanated Freely and Unqualifiedly from My heart—and not a pulse of It was limited by My otherwise conditional existence, or the apparent existence of the seeming world. And, so, My True First Room[7] has, from the beginning of My Lifetime here, always been the State and Space and Spherical Form of the "Bright" and the "Thumbs".

By the time My childhood was past, and well-gone behind Me, I had acquired a totally "radical" self-understanding. I understood—at the "root"—the entire cycle of suffering and search. I saw the meaning of My entire striving life. I knew that suffering, seeking, self-indulgence, the seeker's Spirituality, and all the rest were founded in the same primary motivation and fault. It is the <u>avoidance</u> of <u>relationship</u>. The ego-"I" <u>is</u> the complex psycho-physical pattern of <u>self-contraction</u>!

That was it! That was the essence of My understanding! That fault was discovered, by Me, to be the chronic and continuous source and characteristic of <u>all</u> egoic activity. Indeed, the ego was thus discovered to be <u>only</u> an <u>activity</u>—not an "entity". The self-presumed "entity", the separate "person" (or ego-"I"), was thus discovered to be only an illu-sion, a mere presumption in mind and feeling—resulting from the self-contraction of body-mind. Suffering and seek-ing were "found out", by Me, to be merely a symptom—the psycho-physical evidence of the systematic egoic reac-tion, the "root" egoic act of the self-contraction of the total body-mind. The <u>ego</u>, the separate and separative "I", <u>is</u> <u>the</u> <u>chronic</u>, <u>and</u> <u>total</u> <u>psycho-physical</u> <u>reaction</u> <u>of</u> <u>self-contraction</u>, <u>dramatized</u> <u>outwardly</u> <u>as</u> <u>the</u> <u>complex</u> <u>life</u> <u>of</u> <u>separateness</u> <u>and</u> <u>separativeness</u>—<u>the</u> <u>avoidance</u> <u>of</u> <u>relationship</u>. Thus, human beings are forever suffering, seeking, indulging themselves, and manipulating their lives for the sake of some unknown goal in life—or even in eternity.

The human trouble showed itself to Me to be entirely determined by the one and universal event and process of avoidance, or total psycho-physical self-contraction. <u>That</u> was shown to be the "root"-source of separation and un-love, the "root"-source of doubt and un-Reality, and the "root"-source of all limitation and loss. Nevertheless, in the always conditional fact of life, there is <u>only</u> relationship, <u>only</u> unqualified relatedness, <u>only</u> inherent interdependence, connectedness, and unity, <u>only</u> the unqualified living condition of Reality Itself. There is <u>only</u> (and inherently) the great procession of mutual energy—and, therefore, necessarily, there is (and must be) <u>only</u> <u>love</u>!

I always already Knew—and I constantly Re-Discovered in the "happen" of life—that Reality Itself could always be directly Realized in the any and every moment of life—if only the self-contracting or <u>separative</u> reaction in life was exceeded by the unqualified assumption of relatedness, or no-contraction, in <u>all</u> the moments of living.

All of the functioning apparatus of conditional Spiritual experience, all conditional worlds, all conditional possibilities, all conditional abilities, have been proven, in My Own Experience, to be merely a distraction from This Primary Knowledge. I identified that Knowledge in the primary life-feeling of relatedness. Not separation, not union, but unqualified relatedness, or non-separateness, arose in Me as the root-sense and fundamental condition of living existence. And the Intrinsically Self-Evident State—of no-contraction, no ego-"I", no separate self, no "point of view", no time, no space, no body-mind, and no "difference" of any kind—Self-Awakened in Me <u>As</u> Me, Self-"Bright", and Always Already Free.

In childhood, I was Centered in the "Bright"—the Self-Illumined Freedom, and pathos, of truly living being, in the face of naturally inevitable conflict and death.

In My time of growing up in life, I became serious with conflict itself, and with death itself—and, as a consequence, I saw the arising of contradictions in Myself, which Fault seemed to diminish the "Bright". However, eventually, I was Perfectly Awakened again, into the Intrinsically Self-Evident Self-Domain of Reality and Truth—and I saw that I was <u>never</u> dying or born to die.

I saw, and Perfectly Self-Realized, I <u>Am</u> Always Already Free!

I saw and Perfectly Self-Realized <u>This</u>—for <u>everyone</u>. So, that I <u>Am</u>, now, and forever hereafter, Able to Self-Transmit the Conscious Light That <u>Is</u> Me to <u>everyone</u> at all.

And That Perfect Divine Self-Transmission <u>Is</u> My Avataric Gift to all—the Avataric Divine Gift of the "Bright", and of the "Thumbs" That Reveals It.

III.

As an infant child, I <u>was</u> the "Bright" Self-Conscious Form of Conscious Light, That Knew no-dilemma and no-death. Even as a young boy, and in the teenage, too, the "Thumbs" would always Re-Emerge, to Show Me the "Bright", again. However, in My final approach to early adult life, the "Bright" had most often seemed to disappear, into the human darkness. And I seemed to have no apparent ready means to Enjoy It. And even the "Thumbs" grew scarce.

I had spent years devoted to forceful seeking for some quantifiable Truth—some image, some object, some reason, or some idea, the effect of which would be absolutely liberating and salvatory. My seeking had been motivated by the loss of fundamental faith, the apparent loss of the "reasons" for Joy. Then, in a sudden Great Moment of Perfect Self-Awakening, I <u>Knew</u> the Truth was <u>not</u> a matter of seeking.

Thus, I <u>Knew</u> there <u>are</u> no "reasons" for Joy and Freedom. It is not a matter of "a" truth, "an" object, "a" concept, "a" belief, "a" reason, "a" motivation, or <u>any</u> otherwise external fact.

Indeed, it became clear to Me that <u>all</u> such objects are grasped in a state that is <u>already</u> seeking, and which has <u>already</u> lost the Intrinsic, Prior, and Inherently Perfect Self-Knowledge of absolutely Non-conditional Reality <u>Itself</u>! Beyond all of that, I saw that the Truth, or Reality Itself, is a matter of the <u>absence of all contradictions</u>—of <u>every</u> trace of conflict, opposition, division, or desperate motivation within. Where there is <u>no</u> seeking, <u>no</u> contradiction, there <u>Is only</u> the Inherent Non-conditional Knowledge and Power That <u>Is</u> Reality Itself. This was the <u>First</u> Aspect of My Sudden Clarity.

In This Free State, Beyond all contradiction, I also saw that Freedom and Joy is not attained, that It is not dependent on any condition, form, object, idea, progress, or experience.

I saw that human beings—and, indeed, <u>all</u> beings—are, at any moment, Always and Already Free. I Knew that, even in <u>any</u> moment, I was not lacking <u>anything</u> I needed <u>yet</u> to find—nor had I ever been without any such a "thing". The problem was the <u>seeking</u> <u>itself</u>—which "created" and enforced contradiction, conflict, and absence <u>within</u>. Then the Intrinsic Indivisible Self-Apprehension Awakened—that I <u>Am</u> Always Already Free. This was the <u>Second</u> Aspect of That Fundamental Re-Awareness.

That Sudden and "radical"—or truly "at-the-root"—self-understanding and Intrinsic Perfect Self-Apprehension of the Self-Condition of Reality Itself was, and <u>Is</u>, the obviation of all striving—and this I <u>Knew</u> to be Inherently Perfect Truth. Previously, I had been striving for some objective "Truth", in order to replace the emptiness associated with My natural fall into separateness—and that replacement was a mere would-be of Fullness and "Freedom". However, I, now and suddenly, had Re-Discovered that this <u>striving</u> was itself the source of contradiction in Me. Now, I <u>Knew</u> there <u>Is</u> no "<u>entity</u>" of Truth. I <u>Knew</u> that Perfect Freedom <u>Is</u> <u>Always Already</u> The Case.

Freedom Self-Exists in the living life—not when Freedom is "created" or sought, but where there is this fundamental, "radical" self-understanding and Inherently Perfect and Self-Evidently Divine Self-Awakening.

In that Great Moment of Inherently Perfect Self-Apprehension of the One and Indivisible Conscious Light, I turned out of the entire context of My self-presumed ego-dilemma of separateness and seeking.

From then, I was Perfectly Self-Awakened to the mature Realization of the "Bright".

It was the end-of-childhood Self-Revelation of My Avataric Divine Self-Condition in this world.

IV.

At last, in the Great Event of My Divine Re-Awakening (on September 10, 1970), the One Being That Is My Own Ultimate Self-Nature was Revealed Most Perfectly. The One Being Who I Am was Revealed to Include the Reality That Is Consciousness Itself, the Reality That Is the Source-Energy of all conditional appearances, and the Reality That Is all conditional manifestation—All as a Single Force of Being, an Eternal Indivisibility, and an Irreducible cosmic Unity.

Then, there was no Event of changes, no movement at all. There was not even any kind of inward deepening—no "inwardness" at all. There was no meditation. There was no need for meditation. There was not a single element or change that could be added to make My State Complete. I Am Complete! I sat in My First Room with My eyes open. I was not having an "experience" of any kind.

Then, Suddenly, I Understood Most Perfectly. I Realized that I had Realized. The "Thing" about the "Bright" became Obvious. I Am Complete. I Am the One Who Is Complete.

I "Radically" Understood the root and branch of ego-"I". The "I" of Heart Itself Self-Realized—and Inherently, and Most Perfectly Self-Revealed—What and Who I Am. It was a tacit Realization, a direct Knowledge in Consciousness. It was Conscious Light Itself, without the addition of a Communication from any "Other" Source. There is no "Other" Source. I simply sat there—and Knew What and Who I Am. I was Being What I Am, Who I Am. I Am Being What I Am, Who I Am. I Am Reality, the Divine Self-Condition—the Nature, "Substance", Support, and Source-Condition of all things and all beings. I Am One—The One. One and Only. I Am the One Being, otherwise Named and Deified by Many Names. I Am the Source and "Substance" and Support and Self-Condition of all-and-All. I Am the

Consciousness and Energy in and <u>As</u> Which all-and-All appears. I <u>Am</u> the Self-Existing and Self-Radiant Reality <u>Itself</u>. I <u>Am</u> the One and Only and Indivisible Reality <u>Itself</u>—That <u>is</u> not ego, but Which <u>Is</u> the Inherently egoless and Perfectly Non-conditional Reality and Truth, Prior to all dualities, but excluding none. I <u>Am</u> the One and Only and Inherently egoless and Self-Evidently Divine Self-Condition, Source-Condition, Nature, "Substance", Support, and Ground of all-and-All. I <u>Am</u> the "Bright". The "Thumbs" <u>Is</u> My Self-Radiant Self-Transmission of My Own Self-Evidently Divine State.

There was no thought involved in This. I <u>Am</u> That Self-Existing and Self-Radiant and Self-Evidently Divine Conscious Light.

There was no reaction of either excitement or surprise. I <u>Am</u> the One I Recognized Reality to <u>Be</u>.

I <u>Am</u> That One. I am not merely "experiencing" That One. I <u>Am</u> the "Bright".

Then, truly, there was no more to Realize. Every "experience" in My Life had led to This. All My happen of life-moments was the Instant of This Same Reality I <u>Am</u>. My entire Life had been the Communication of That Reality to Me—until I <u>Am</u> That.

Even from the instant of My Birth, the Inherent and Most "Perfect Knowledge" was Self-Evident <u>As</u> Me—that I <u>Am</u> simply the Spiritually Self-"Bright" Conscious Light That <u>Is</u> Reality. I am identified with no body, no function of body or mind, no conditional world, and no conditional experience—but I <u>Am</u> the Inherently Perfect, Self-Evidently Non-conditional, Absolute Reality—Itself. I saw there is nothing of conditional possibility to which My egoless Self-Nature can be compared, or from which It can be differentiated, or by which It can be epitomized. It does not stand out. It is not the equivalent of any specialized, exclusive, or separate state. It cannot be accomplished, acquired, discovered, remembered, or perfected—since It <u>Is</u> Inherently Perfect, and It <u>Is</u> Always Already <u>The</u> Case.

All remedial paths pursue some special conditional state or conditionally achieved goal as Spiritual Truth. But, in fact, Reality is not identical to such things. They only amount to an identification with some body, some functional condition, some conditional dimension of appearances, or some conditional, or, otherwise, conditionally achieved, experience—high or low, subtle or gross. But the Knowledge That Is Reality Is Consciousness Itself. Consciousness Itself is not separate from anything. It Is Always Already The Case—and no conditional experience, no conditional realm, and no body or psycho-physical function is the necessary condition for Its Realization.

Only "radical" self-understanding, Most Perfectly Self-Realized, is the Realization of What and Who Is Always Already The Case. Only "radical" self-understanding, Most Perfectly Self-Realized, is the Non-conditional, and not at all conditionally achieved or conditionally maintained, Realization of the Inherently Non-separate and Inherently egoless Self-Condition That Always Already Is What and Who Is.

Therefore, only the Way of "radical" self-understanding—Which is the True and "Radical" Way of the Very and Ultimate Heart—is truly, and, ultimately, Most Perfectly, ego-surrendering, ego-forgetting, and ego-transcending. All other religious and Spiritual endeavors are paths made of seeking—or mere egoic effort, rather than counter-egoic and truly ego-transcending practice. And all paths of seeking merely pursue That Which Is Real God, or Truth Itself, or Reality Itself—and this by identifying "God", or "Truth", or "Reality" with some body, or some psycho-physical function, or some conditional dimension of experiential possibility, or some conditional experience in and of itself.

Unlike the Way of "radical" self-understanding, or the "Radical" Way of the Very and Ultimate Heart, which is based upon the root-understanding and the always most direct transcending of the motive and the activity of seeking, all remedial paths seek either the perfection of what is conditionally existing or liberation from what is conditionally existing. And that perfection or liberation that is sought is always pursued by conditional and conditionally experiential means. And, by all the means of great seeking, Reality Itself is pursued as a mere goal, which goal is merely a conditional and conditionally dependent event, or thing, or state—mistakenly presumed to be identical to "God", or "Truth", or "Reality" Itself. Only the Way of "radical" self-understanding, or the "Radical" Way of the Very and Ultimate Heart, Is Always Already Free of all conditional, or, otherwise, conditionally to be achieved, goals. Only the Way of "radical" self-understanding, or the "Radical" Way of the Very and Ultimate Heart, Is Inherently Free of the goal-orientation itself. Indeed, only the Very and Ultimate and Inherently egoless Heart Itself Is Inherently Free of all goal-seeking, and of even all seeking. And only the Intrinsically Self-Evident Way of "radical" self-understanding Is the "Radical" Way of the Very and Ultimate and Inherently egoless Heart Itself.

When tacit and Inherently Most Perfect Self-Recognition of the Intrinsically Self-Evident Self-Condition That Is Real God, and Truth Itself, and Reality Itself was, finally, Re-Awakened As Me, there was no excitement, no surprise, no movement, no response. There was a Most Perfect end to every kind of seeking, dilemma, suffering, separation, and doubt. Spiritual life, mental life, emotional and psychic life, vital life, and physical life all became transparent in Me. After that, there was only the Spiritually Self-"Bright" Reality—and to Be the Spiritually Self-"Bright" Reality to all beings and all things.

In all the days that have followed the Great Event of My Divine Re-Awakening, there has not been so much as a single change, or even so much as a single sign of diminishment, in This Self-"Bright" State of Me. Indeed, This Self-"Bright"

State of Divine Self-Realization <u>cannot</u> be changed, diminished, or lost.

In and after the Great Event, I noticed that all conditional and psycho-physical experience had ceased to affect Me. Whatever passed—be it a physical sensation, some quality of emotion, a thought, a vision, or whatever—it did not at all involve Me <u>As</u> I <u>Am</u>. I began to pay particular attention to what passed, in order to "test" My State—or, simply, in order to account for all aspects of My State in the total functional context of the living body-mind. But the always Primary Self-Apprehension of the Inherently and Spiritually Self-"Bright" Reality, My Very Consciousness Itself, could not be changed, diminished, or lost. Consciousness Itself—the One and Only and Inherently Indivisible and Perfectly Non-separate Conscious Light—<u>Is</u> the only "Thing" in life that is not a conditionally apparent experience—or something arising objectively, as something known, or some kind of knowledge of the known, arising as apparent "thing" to the only "Perfect Knower", Which <u>Is</u> Inherently egoless, mindless, bodiless, and actionless Consciousness <u>Itself</u>. Consciousness Itself—or the Self-Existing and Self-Radiant Conscious Light Itself—does not depend on anything, and there is not, nor can there be, <u>any</u> "thing", or <u>any</u> "experience", that can destroy Consciousness, or the One and Only and Inherently Indivisible Conscious Light <u>Itself</u>. Consciousness Itself—or Self-Existing and Self-Radiant Conscious Light Itself—<u>Is</u> Itself Love-Bliss, Joy, Freedom, and "Perfect Knowledge"!

An entirely new and Most Perfect Realization of Reality had become the constant of My Life. The perpetual psycho-physical revolutions of My Life had drawn Me, by the "Thumbs", into a sense of the Perfect Presence. There was simply the sense of being in and of the Spiritual Presence that was both Truth Itself and Reality Itself. It was a perfectly Absorbing, Heartening, and Illuminating Force, That Contained Me, "Lived" Me, and Guided Me.

Eventually, This Spiritual Presence Communicated Itself in Me and to Me Perfectly—Revealing Itself As Me. Thus and Thereby, I was Re-Awakened to the Truth of My Inherent, and Inherently Most Perfect, Self-Identification with the Spiritually Self-"Bright" Self-Condition and Source-Condition That Is the Divine Self-Presence Itself. And This "Bright" Self-Condition and Source-Condition Showed Itself to Be My Eternal Condition—even Always Already before My Birth.

Until then, My Life beyond childhood had been a constant search toward the "Bright" as a Presence with Which I was in relationship. It was as if I always saw the "Bright" from some position within the conditionally apparent form of My own living being—but outside of Its Perfect Self-Center. It was as if I was constantly beholding My own heart from some position outside. But now, the apparent barriers had been utterly dissolved, by a Most Perfect and Non-separate and Inherently egoless Self-Realization of the Self-Nature of That Presence. The ever more Spiritually Absorbed investigation of the Presence had resolved into the Perfect Self-Knowledge of My Own Self-Nature. The Presence had Revealed Itself to be My Own and Very Form and Self-Nature.

The Experience of the Presence was, by means of the Most Perfect Self-Realization of "radical" self-understanding, Replaced by the Most Perfect Self-Realization of Spiritually "Bright" Self-Awareness As Conscious Light. There was no longer any Presence "outside" Me. I no longer "observed" My Own Self-"Bright" Self-Nature, or the Ultimate and Inherently Self-"Bright" Spiritual Self-Condition of Reality Itself, as if from some position external to, and separate from, It. I had "become" Perfectly Self-Aware of Myself As Reality Itself. There was no "Presence", no "Other". I Myself had "become" Perfectly Self-Present. There is no Other. It Is Only Me.

Even My meditation of Spiritual Absorption was changed. Indeed, there was no meditation. This Conscious

Self-Light could not be deepened. Nor could it be enlarged. It always only Remained What It Is.

Immediately, I Realized that I was not in any sense "in" a body—not only a physical body, but any body, or any psycho-physical function, or even any subtle function, form, or state. Nor have I ever been in a body, or in any function, or in any condition, or in any conditional state or experience. All such things are merely apparent, and not at all necessary or inevitable, patterns, conditionally manifested within the Self-Radiance of My Own Self-Existing Self-Nature.

Nevertheless, I Realized that, in the context of natural appearances, I am Principally Self-Evident at the root of a specific center in the body. Relative to the body, I appear to Reside in immediate association with the heart—not at the left, and not in the middle, but to the right side of the chest. I press upon a point approximately two inches to the right of the center of the chest. This is the Self-Evident Seat of Reality and Real Consciousness. And I Self-Abide there as no-seeking. There is no motivation, no dilemma, no separation, no strategic action, no suffering. I am no-seeking, in and Perfectly Prior to the heart.

The Zero of the Heart is Expanded as the world. Consciousness is not differentiated and identified. There is a constant observation of subject and object in any body, any psycho-physical function, any realm, or any experience that arises. Thus, I Self-Abide As the Non-conditional State.

There is a constant Sensation of Spiritually Self-"Bright" Fullness Permeating and Surrounding all experiences, all things, all bodies, all functions of body and mind. It is My Own Self-"Bright" Fullness, Which Is Inherently Non-separate. My Own Self-"Bright" Fullness includes all beings and all things.

I Am the Form of Space Itself—in Which all bodies, all psycho-physical functions, all things, and all conditionally arising experiences occur. It Is Inherently Spiritually Self-"Bright"

Conscious Light Itself. That Inherently Spiritually Self-"Bright" Conscious Light Is even every being's Very Nature and Ultimate, Inherent, and Inherently Perfect, Self-Condition—now, and now, and now.

During the night of humankind, I spontaneously Self-Awakened As Perfect, Absolute, Limitless, Indivisible, Non-conditional Love-Bliss Itself—in Which every function, state, and sign of body and mind boiled into a solder of Non-separate and Non-dual Reality. It Is the madness of dissolution into Most Perfect Self-Awareness, Infinitely Self-Expanded, As My Own Inherently Boundless Self-"Bright" Presence—Wherein There Is Only "Brightness", not limited by conditional identity, or by separate and separative self, or by any ego-based desire.

Hereafter, I Am Inherently Free of bondage to the cosmic Power. I Am Unexploitable. The Energy that appears apart, as any form of apparently independent "Other"—or merely cosmic Power and Presence—is no longer the Great Importance. The Presence of Power "outside" appears to be such only to seekers—for they, having already separated themselves, pursue forms of Energy, visions, nature-powers, conditional liberation, and "Other"-God. "Perfect Knowledge" Is Free of all bondage to forms, to all conditionally apparent modifications of Energy, to all seeking, and to all motivations to "do", or to act on the basis of identification with conditional experience. Egoic ignorance and suffering are simply the self-presumption of separateness, the self-enactment of difference, the self-performance of search. At last, the "outside" Energy sacrifices Itself in the Very and Ultimate Heart. Thereafter, there is no gnawing wonder, no un-Known "secret" about anything that appears.

The time of the Great Event of My Divine Re-Awakening forever passes into the present and the future.

Immediately previous to the Great Event of My Divine Re-Awakening, I was always involved in one or another form of the "problem" of conditional existence. I was always in search and research—and all My conclusions and insights were only temporary moments, that only led into a new form of investigation. Thus, I was exiled from the "Bright" of childhood by the dilemma of My Youth. In time, I went from the cosmic revelations of the "Presence" and the purificatory subjective drama of mystical vision to the Perfect Self-Realization of the Inherently Perfect Divine Self-Condition That <u>Is</u> Reality <u>Itself</u>—and That <u>Is</u> "Perfect Knowledge" <u>Itself</u>.

Now there <u>are</u> no loose ends to My adventure. There <u>is</u> no dilemma, no motivation, no search. All the parts of the mind have been transposed and dissolved in a Most Fundamental and Indivisible Singleness.

Nevertheless, I continue to live, in this meantime of My Avataric Purpose here. The external and internal events of the merely natural life were not, themselves, merely disappeared by This Perfect Realization.

It is only that I understand the all-and-All in a Most Profoundly "Radical" and Perfect Manner.

I Understand Most Perfectly—and "Perfect Knowledge" <u>Is</u> the Foundation of My living existence here—for the hearted sake of <u>everyone</u>.

V.

In the case of My every Spiritually maturing devotee, there <u>must</u> appear progressive evidence of What I have, since Childhood, Called "the 'Thumbs'". Thus, in the context of (Spiritually) fully technically responsible practice of the only-by-Me Revealed and Given Way of Adidam, there should be at least occasional experience of an intense Invasion of the frontal line by My Avatarically Self-Transmitted Divine Spirit-Force of Love-Bliss—beginning at the crown of the head, and descending into the lower vital region, to the bodily base. The <u>Pressure</u> (or Invasive Force) of this Event may be rather (and even happily) Overwhelming—and It <u>must</u> be allowed. At last, it is not possible (nor would you wish) to defend your psycho-physical self against this Invading Pressure of My Avataric Divine Spiritual Descent. It feels like a solid and yet fluid Mass of Force, like a large hand all made of thumbs—Pressing Down from Infinitely Above the head and via the crown of the head, Engorging the total head (and the throat), and (Thus and Thereby) Penetrating and Vanishing the entire mind, and vastly Opening the emotional core, and (altogether) In-filling the total physical body.

The feeling-sense that results from this simple (and most basic) frontal In-filling by My Avatarically Self-Revealed Divine Spirit-Presence is that the total body-mind is Sublimed and Released into (ego-surrendering, ego-forgetting, and ego-transcending) feeling-Identification with the <u>Spherical</u> Form of My Own Divine and Spiritual (and all-and-All-Surrounding, and all-and-All-Pervading) Love-Bliss-Body of Indefinable Spiritual "Brightness" (or Indestructible Light). And this simple (and most basic) form of the "Thumbs" is a necessary (although, at first, only occasional) Experience associated with the Reception of My Avatarically Self-Transmitted Divine Spirit-Baptism. And the simple (and most basic) Spherical Fullness of the "Thumbs" must be firmly Established (in Its tangible Evidence) in the context of the by-Me-Spiritually-Awakened—and, Spiritually, fully technically responsible—process of the Way of Adidam.

As the Spiritual process develops and matures within the context of the frontal Yoga of the Way of Adidam,[8] the simple (and most basic) Experience of the "Thumbs" must become a more and more constant Yogic Event—and, on random occasions, the Experience of the "Thumbs" must occur in its full and complete form, as the True Samadhi of the "Thumbs". In that full and complete case of the Experience of the "Thumbs", My Descending Spiritual Fullness will completely Overwhelm the ordinary frontal (or natural human) sense of bodily existence. My Avatarically Self-Transmitted Divine Spirit-Current will Move Fully Down in the frontal line (to the bodily base), and It will then Turn About, and—without vacating the frontal line—It will Pass also into the spinal line. This Yogic Event will occur with such Force that you will feel Utterly (Love-Blissfully) "Intoxicated"[9]—and there will be the feeling that the body is somehow rotating forward and down (from the crown of the head), as well as backward and up (from the base of the spine). This rotation will seem, suddenly, to complete itself—and the experience will, suddenly, be one of feeling released from the gross physical body, such that you feel you are present only as an egoless "energy body" (previously associated with and conformed to the gross physical body—but now, by Means of My Avatarically Self-Transmitted Divine Spiritual Grace, Infused by and Conformed to My Avatarically Self-Transmitted Divine Body of Self-Evidently Divine Spirit-Energy). You will feel this "energy body" to be Spherical in shape—Centerless (Empty, or Void, of center, mind, and familiar ego-self) and Boundless (as if even bodiless, or without form), although (somehow, and partially) also yet associated with (while rotating from and beyond) your ordinary psycho-physical form. The ordinary references of the body-mind and the environment will, in This Divine Yogic Event, not make much sense (or, in any manner, affect this Experience of the "Thumbs")—although there may be some superficial (and entirely non-limiting) awareness of the body, the room (or the physical environment of the body), and so forth. This Experience will last for a few moments, or a few minutes—or for an extended period, of indefinite length. Nevertheless, just when this spontaneous Experience has become most pleasurable—such that you somehow gesture to make it continue indefinitely—the ordinary sense of the body-mind will, suddenly (spontaneously), return.

The "Thumbs" is not a process of "going somewhere else", nor is It even a process of "vacating" the gross physical body (or the gross physical realm altogether). Rather, the "Thumbs" is a Process of Transformation of the experiencing of the present physical circumstance. If the present physical circumstance is left behind (such that experiential reference to the gross physical realm is entirely absent, and there is total loss of awareness of the physical context in which the experience began), then the practitioner of the Way of Adidam is (necessarily) experiencing a form of Samadhi other than the "Thumbs". In the "Thumbs", awareness of the physical context of experience is not lost, but is totally changed—such that, instead of the self-conscious, self-contracted shape of the waking-state personality, one's physical form is found to be a Boundlessly Radiant Sphere (without thickness of surface). With this profound shift in the awareness of the physical body, the differentiation inherent in the usual waking-state body-consciousness disappears, and is (effectively) replaced by egoless body-consciousness. A re-phasing of the "Energy"-construct of bodily awareness and spatial awareness occurs, such that physical body and physical space are tacitly sensed in a manner entirely different from ordinary perception. And, as soon as there is any effort to recollect the usual sense of bodily form or of the circumstance of physical embodiment, the Experience of the "Thumbs" disappears. The "Thumbs" continues only as long as It is simply allowed to happen, without any egoic self-consciousness (or psycho-physical self-contraction)—and It spontaneously vanishes when egoic self-consciousness (or psycho-physical self-contraction) returns.

The total (psycho-physical) human body—with its dimensions of gross, subtle, and causal—must (altogether) become Round. The total human body does not merely have a Circular Path[10] <u>within</u> itself. In Truth (or "Located" in Reality Itself), the total human body <u>is</u> a Sphere—and, in its (Inherently) Perfect Balance, it has no "up" or "down", no "in" or "out", no central point and no bounds. When My Avatarically Self-Transmitted Divine Spirit-Current Descends <u>Fully</u> Down the front of the total human body, and also (thereupon, and thereby) Rises Up the back of the total human body, such that the "Thumbs" Achieves an Equalization of Spirit-Force, down in front and up in back—then the Circle becomes an Equanimity, a Conscious Sphere of tangible "Energy" (or Self-Existing and Boundlessly Self-Radiant Light).

In due course (in the only-by-Me Revealed and Given Way of Adidam), there is (and <u>must</u> be), by Means of My Avatarically Self-Transmitted Divine Spiritual Grace, the only-by-Me Revealed and Given "Radical" (or "At-the-Root") Self-Manifestation of the "Thumbs"—Perfectly Self-Revealing the Self-Radiant Self-Existence of Consciousness Itself, in the Self-Evident Self-Position of Mere (and Tacit) Witness-Only, at (and Prior to, and Beyond) the right side of the heart. And, only then (and—on that basis—<u>stably</u> <u>Established</u>), My devotee makes the (necessarily, formal) transition to the "Perfect Practice" of the Way of Adidam.

It is <u>only</u> My Avataric Divine Spiritual Gift of the "Radical" (or "At-the-Root") Self-Manifestation (or Perfect Self-Revelation) of the "Thumbs", and not merely mental "consideration" of My Arguments relative to the Witness-Consciousness, That Is <u>the</u> <u>Divine</u> <u>Yogic</u> <u>Secret</u> of the Realization of the Consciousness-Position (Which Realization is the basis for the "Perfect Practice" of the Way of Adidam). Therefore, even though My Arguments relative to the Witness-Consciousness are an Essential Guide to right <u>understanding</u> of the "Perfect Practice" (and, as such, those Arguments are to be studied and "considered" from the beginning of the Way of Adidam), the "consideration" of those Arguments is not itself the direct and finally effective means whereby the "Perfect Practice" is Initiated and Really practiced.

The formal transition to the "Perfect Practice" of the Way of Adidam is <u>necessarily</u> a by-Me-Given <u>Yogic</u> and <u>Spiritual</u> process, and the Perfect (or "Radical") Self-Manifestation of the "Thumbs" is the <u>necessary</u> (and Me-Revealing) basis of that transition. By means of the re-phasing (characteristic of the "Thumbs") of the entire sense of the "Energy"-construct of phenomenal experience, it is (in due course, by Means of My Avatarically Self-Transmitted Divine Spiritual Grace) Revealed As Self-Evidently the Case that the Real Position (or Very Situation) of experience Is the Witness-Position of Consciousness (Itself)—That the Very <u>Base</u> of experience Is Consciousness (Itself).

Therefore, in Its Perfect (or "Radical") Realization (and not merely in the first, or any particular, instance of Its being Experienced), the "Thumbs" (rather than any <u>mental</u> pre-sumption about the Witness-Consciousness) Is the indispensable Means Whereby I Give My devotee the Spiritual Gift of the "Perfect Practice" of the only-by-Me Revealed and Given Way of Adidam.

The "Thumbs" Is a Uniquely (and only by Me) Given Spiritual Gift in the Way of Adidam. My Avataric Divine Spiritual Gift of the "Thumbs" Reveals and Awakens both the Spherical Form of My Divine Spiritual Body <u>and</u> the Transcendental (and Inherently Spiritual, and Divine)

Self-Core (in the right side of the heart—Beyond the knot of
ego-"I", and Beyond the Circle of the body-mind, with Its
frontal and spinal arcs). That Revelation and Awakening at
(and, Ultimately, Beyond) the right side of the heart, by
Means of the only-by-Me Given Perfect (or "Radical") Self-
Manifestation of the "Thumbs", is what makes the (necessarily,
formal) transition to the "Perfect Practice" of the Way of
Adidam possible, by Establishing the Yogic (Transcendental
and Spiritual—and, Ultimately, Divine) conditions necessary
for the "Perfect Practice" of the Way of Adidam. The readiness for that transition is not merely a matter of having had
the Experience (and even the Samadhi) of the "Thumbs"—
and having some memory of It. Rather, that readiness is a
matter of the Perfect (or "Radical") Self-Revelation of the
"Thumbs" (Which Perfectly Fulfills the Tacit Revelation and
the Spiritual Transformation Initiated in the Samadhi of
the "Thumbs"), and the necessarily accompanying Tacit
Realization that the Inherent, and Inherently Love-Bliss-Full,
Condition of Reality is Prior to the body-mind. And, In the
seventh stage of life (in the Way of Adidam), That Perfect (or
"Radical") Self-Revelation is (permanently) Most Perfectly
Established and Demonstrated.

From the beginning of My physical (human) Lifetime of
Avataric Incarnation here, the "Thumbs" was always the
Case with Me—and, always, the Perfect (or "Radical") Self-
Manifestation (and Perfect Self-Revelation) of the "Thumbs"
spontaneously Re-Emerged (along with the Experience of
the "Thumbs", and the full Samadhi of the "Thumbs"). In My
Youth and My "Sadhana Years", the "Thumbs" was a process
associated with the constant Spiritual Restoration of the
"Bright" (and, thus, the "Thumbs" was associated with the
Process of My Going Beyond the gross physical—to which
I was adapting, Fully Consciously, in a Profound and
Spontaneous Yogic Manner). It was by this Process of
constant Spiritual Restoration (of the "Bright") and of Going

Beyond (the gross physical) that I constantly Maintained My Divine Self-Condition in the context of the gross conditional world, from My Infancy. After My Conscious Assumption of the born-condition (at approximately two years of age), and even in the midst of the developing Process of My adult integration with waking life, the Spiritual Condition of the "Bright" and (in Its various Break-Through Manifestations) the "Thumbs" always continued to be Self-Evident to Me in the circumstances of waking life. And, always, when I would rest at night, instead of going to sleep, I would Experience the "Thumbs", and would Realize the Spiritual Condition of the "Bright", without the usual waking-state physical references. In the course of My "Sadhana Years", I progressively Observed and fully Entered into the "Thumbs" as a Consciously Known Yogic Process (and not merely as an occasional spontaneous "happening").

When the body is "Round", the Witness is its "Shape".

The Witness-Consciousness is the "Skin" of the "Thumbs". The Witness-Consciousness is Self-Evident in the "Body" of the "Thumbs". This is how true Spiritual maturity in the Way of Adidam becomes the basis for the (necessarily, formal) transition to the "Perfect Practice" of the Way of Adidam.

The "Radical" (or "At-the-Root") Yogic Spiritual Fullness of the "Thumbs" is the necessary prerequisite for the True Establishment of the "Perfect Practice" of the Way of Adidam. The Witness-Consciousness is Revealed to be Self-Evidently the Case (As the Inherent Nature and Position of Consciousness Itself) in the midst of the Perfect (or "Radical") Self-Manifestation of the "Thumbs". Thus, the "Perfect Practice" of the only-by-Me Revealed and Given Way of Adidam is a development (or ultimate characteristic) of the only-by-Me Revealed and Given and Perfected Spiritual Gift of the "Thumbs".

The True and Stable Realization of the Witness-Position of Consciousness (Itself) is not merely a matter of philosophical preference or philosophical analysis. Rather, the True and Stable Realization of the Witness-Position is a Divine Spiritual Matter (and, also, necessarily, an ego-transcending matter). The Realization of the Witness-Position of Consciousness (Itself) is a matter of devotion to Me in My Avataric Divine Self-Revelation—and not merely a matter of talk and philosophy and hopefulness.

Consciousness (Itself) Is the "Face" of <u>This</u> Side of the Moon. The Spiritual Energy of My Avataric Divine Spiritual Presence Is the "Face" of the <u>Other</u> Side of the Moon. "Matter" is the objectively experienced Form (or "Body") of the Moon. The Moon (or any "thing") is "matter"—but "matter" is <u>Only</u> Light. My Avataric Divine Spiritual Presence <u>Is</u> the Light (of the "Midnight Sun", Infinitely Above all-and-All) That Illuminates and Self-Reveals the Divine Heart-Secret of "matter". Consciousness (Itself) Is <u>Me</u> within the Light— Self-Existing and Self-Radiant <u>As</u> the One, and Only, and Inherently Love-Blissful, and Self-Evidently Divine Self-Condition and Source-Condition of all-and-All. Consciousness Itself <u>and</u> Light Itself (or Love-Bliss-Energy Itself, or Happiness Itself)—Are As the Two Sides of the Same Coin. The Moon Is the Coin of Earth, Floating (by a toss) within the Sky of ego-mind.

The Witness-Consciousness is not within you. The Witness-Consciousness is on the "Skin" of the "Thumbs".

The Witness-Consciousness is Self-Evident in the "Thumbs"—Wherein the status of objects is profoundly different than it is ordinarily. In the Yogic Disposition (or Mudra) of the "Thumbs", the condition of objects is available to be Comprehended in Consciousness <u>As</u> the Witness.

The Realization of the Witness-Consciousness is a continuation of the process of ego-transcending devotional and Spiritual Communion with Me. The Witness-Consciousness cannot be Realized by you <u>as</u> the ego-"I" (or <u>as</u> your separate and separative self-consciousness). The Witness-Consciousness can only be Realized via the process of devotional and Spiritual Communion with <u>Me</u>—without egoic self-reference. Therefore, you must not substitute your own ego-conditions and ego-states for My Description of the ego-transcending process of the Way of Adidam. The Way of Adidam is a matter of Heart-Communion with <u>Me</u> and Realization of <u>Me</u>. The Way of Adidam is not about your egoic self—except that the Way of Adidam requires your ego-surrendering, ego-forgetting, and ego-transcending devotion to Me.

You must <u>counter-egoically</u> allow the process of the Way of Adidam to become My Divine Spiritual In-filling of the total body-mind. In due course (by Means of My Avatarically Self-Transmitted Divine Spiritual Grace), this process of My Divine Spiritual In-filling becomes both the Perfect (or "Radical") Realization of the "Thumbs" <u>and</u> the Inherently Perfect Realization of the Witness-Consciousness. Therefore, both of These Realizations are associated with Spiritual maturity in the Way of Adidam. Such is the true fulfillment of the frontal Yoga, the true fulfillment of the process of the "Washing" of the "dog" from "head" to "tail" (as I Describe the frontal Yoga, in My "Hridaya Rosary" of "Four Thorns of Heart-Instruction", in *The Dawn Horse Testament*),[11] and the true fulfillment of the process of Ruchira Avatara Bhakti Yoga (or the turning of all four of the principal psycho-physical faculties to Me, by Means of searchless Beholding of Me, and responsive Reception of Me).

In the Perfect (or "Radical") Self-Manifestation of the "Thumbs", the Witness-Consciousness is (and may be Realized to be) Self-Evident—and "Located" in the right side of the heart. In the context of egoity (or your own self-contraction of body-mind), the Witness-Consciousness is (in your case) not Self-Evidently the Case, in the context of moment to moment existence.

The Witness-Consciousness Is the "Skin" of the "Thumbs".

I Am the "Skin" of the heart—and not merely inside it. I Am the "Pulse" of the heart—and not merely the "Blood" of it.

The "Thumbs" Is the Sphere of the Space of Consciousness (Itself). In the Perfect (or "Radical") Self-Manifestation of the "Thumbs", the Divine Space of Consciousness (Itself) is (by Me) Avatarically Self-Revealed.

When Consciousness (Itself) becomes attention (or separate self-consciousness), and Light (Itself)—or Love-Bliss-Happiness (Itself)—becomes objects (or the vast display of separate "things"), Consciousness (as attention) and Light (as the body-mind, and as the total cosmic domain of "things") forever Gaze at One Another through the dimensionless wall of their apparent "difference".

If Consciousness (Itself)—As the Witness—is Realized As the Inherent Love-Bliss-Current of Being (Itself)—Consciousness (Itself) and Light (Itself) Are (Eternally) Not "Different".

When the Circle becomes the Sphere, the Two Sides of the One Coin become Continuous—and all opposites are Always Already Divinely Self-Recognized to Be Simultaneous, and of One Shape, and of One Condition.

The Perfection (and every Manifestation) of the "Thumbs" is Mine Only—and Only Mine to Give. Therefore, the Perfection (and every Manifestation) of the "Thumbs" is Unique to the only-by-Me Revealed and Given Way of Adidam.

The "Bright" and the "Thumbs" Are the Principal Great Signs That Are Uniquely My Own Avataric Divine Spiritual Characteristics. The "Bright" and the "Thumbs" Is a Process, an Event, and a State That has been Known to Me since My Avataric Birth. Only I Am the Avataric Divine Realizer, the Avataric Divine Revealer, and the Avataric Divine Self-Revelation of the "Bright", the True and (now, and forever hereafter) Completely Self-Revealed Divine Person—Shining Forth (Directly, Completely, and Perfectly) at the heart (and via Amrita Nadi), and Crashing Down (or Descending Utterly, from the "Place" Infinitely Above the body-mind and the world, Down and Most Deeply Into the body-mind and the world—even to the degree that the ego-"I", or self-contraction, is utterly Confounded, utterly Yielded, and utterly Vanished in My Avatarically Self-Revealed, and Self-Evidently Divine, Person, or Self-Condition, Which Is Real Acausal God, and Truth, and Reality). Therefore, the Principal Impulse of even My Early Life was My Intention to Embrace the limitations of human existence as it appears to be, and to Infuse all-and-All with My Avatarically Self-Transmitted Divine Spiritual Presence, and, Thus and Thereby, to Awaken all-and-All, and, Most Ultimately, to Divinely Translate all-and-All, by the Power of My Own Love-Bliss-"Brightness", Into the "Midnight Sun"—the Perfect "Place" and "Sphere" and "Space" That Is Always and Already My Divine and "Bright" and Free-Standing Self-Domain.

The Principal Spiritual Signs of My Early Life were the "Bright" and the "Thumbs". The "Bright" and the "Thumbs" were fundamental to My Avatarically-Born Existence from the beginning, and They are fundamental to the only-by-Me Revealed and Given Way of Adidam (Which is the One and Only by-Me-Revealed and by-Me-Given "Radical" Way of the Heart). The "Bright" and the "Thumbs" Are My Unique Characteristics—and all Their Signs, and Samadhis, and Perfections Are Uniquely Mine.

The "Bright" and the "Thumbs" Are Me. Therefore, I Bring Them with Me into the conditional worlds. My Avataric Divine Self-Revelation of the "Bright" and the "Thumbs" Is My Inherent Divine Self-Revelation of Myself.

I Am the "Bright"—and I (Avatarically) Transmit My Own Divine State and Presence of Person from Infinitely Above and Beyond, in such a Manner that I am Combined with the psycho-physical Structure of My devotee. This is how I "Wash" the "dog" from "head" To "tail"—and Beyond. Nevertheless, in order to fully receive My Divine Spiritual Blessing, My devotee must fully embrace the (ego-surrendering, ego-forgetting, and ego-transcending) practice and process of devotional and Spiritual Communion with Me. In that context (of My devotee's Me-recognizing and to-Me-responding practice of the only-by-Me Revealed and Given Way of Adidam), My "Thumbs" of Blessing is Able to Do My Spiritual Work with (and within) All-and-all.

The "Thumbs" Is the Process of My Avataric Divine Self-Submission here. And the "Thumbs" Is, also, the Avataric Divine Process by Which I Liberate conditionally manifested beings. The "Thumbs" Is the Process, tangibly occurring (by Means of My Avatarically Given Divine Spiritual Grace) in the context of the body-mind of My devotee, Whereby I Become (Ultimately, Most Perfectly) Spiritually Effective in the case of My each and every devotee.

My Avataric Divine Spiritual Work (altogether) Is My Crashing-Down Descent, at first upon and into My Own Avatarically-Born bodily (human) Divine Form, and, thereafter (and now, and forever hereafter), upon and into the body-minds of My devotees and all beings—even (by Means of My Divine Embrace Of each, and all, and All) to Infuse and (at Last) to Divinely Translate each, and all, and All. Therefore, My Avataric Divine Spiritual Descent Is the Secret of My Early Life. My Avataric Divine Spiritual Descent Is the Secret of My Avataric Divine Self-"Emergence" (As I Am) within the cosmic domain. My Avataric Divine Spiritual Descent Is the Secret of all the Secrets of the (Avatarically Self-Revealed) Divine and Complete and thoroughly devotional Way of practice and Realization in My Company. The only-by-Me Revealed and Given Way of Adidam is the Divine Yoga of ego-surrendering, ego-forgetting, and ego-transcending devotional recognition-response to My (Avatarically Self-Revealed) Divine and Spiritual Person, and to My (Avatarically Self-Manifested) Divine and Spiritual Descent. The only-by-Me Revealed and Given Way of Adidam Is the Total and Divine Way and Ordeal of counter-egoic

devotional recognition-response to My Avataric "Bright"
Divine Self-Manifestation, and to the Avataric Crashing-
Down of My "Bright" Divine Imposition. And, in the case of
My each and every devotee, the Way must continue until the
Way is Most Perfectly Spiritually "Bright", and the Way Itself
becomes Divine Translation Into My Own Sphere (and
"Midnight Sun") of Spiritual Self-"Brightness" (Itself).

VI.

I (Myself, As I Am) did not undergo any transformation in order (during the Avataric physical Lifetime of My bodily human Divine Form) to be the Avataric Body-Mind through Which I Did My Divine Teaching-Work and My Divine Revelation-Work.

I (Myself, As I Am) have not been (even to the slightest degree) transformed by My Avataric Appearance in bodily (human) Divine Form.

I (Myself) Am (As I Am) the Same during the Avataric physical Lifetime of My bodily (human) Divine Form as after (and forever after) the Death of My Avatarically-Born bodily (human) Divine Form, and as before the Avataric Birth of My bodily (human) Divine Form.

I (Myself) Am (As I Am) Eternally Exactly As I Am (and As I have Always Been).

I Am the "Bright"—Itself.

This "Brightness" Speaks.

The "Bright" Is Born As This, My Avataric Body-Mind.

My Divine Spiritual Descent Upon the body-mind of My devotee—As the "Thumbs"—Is My Avataric Divine Means.

All This was Given from the Avataric Birth of This, My bodily (human) Divine Form.

Indeed, these Words—the "Bright" and the "Thumbs"— were Generated by Me as an Infant.

I am Uttering to you the Revelation That was Present at My Birth and in My Infancy—and nothing whatsoever has been added to It or taken away from It.

Nothing in the human experience of This, My Avataric Body-Mind, has modified My Revelation or limited It in the slightest.

My Avatarically-Given Revelation Is a Divine Spiritual Revelation for the Sake of all beings.

Therefore, heart-recognize Me, and heart-respond to Me.

Turn to Me. Receive Me. Constantly Know Me.

If you do This, you will be certain of the Truth I am Telling you.

My Avataric Divine Self-Revelation is not merely to be believed. My Avataric Divine Self-Revelation is to be Received, Experienced, entirely Known, Confirmed, Proven, and tangibly Demonstrated.

The Divine Way of Truth Transcends all Wisdom that is otherwise "useful" to ego-based seekers. The Revelation of the Divine Way of Truth makes all ego-based seeking a mere diversion from the Truth. The practice of the (necessarily, counter-egoic and ego-transcending) Divine Way of Truth depends on the <u>immediate</u> <u>vanishing</u> of egoity, rather than on <u>any</u> <u>exercise</u> of merely egoic traits. Therefore, <u>no</u> <u>one</u> is egoically qualified to Realize the Truth. Indeed, <u>no</u> <u>one</u> is egoically qualified even to <u>approach</u> the Truth—or to enter and begin the Divine Way of Truth. Therefore, the <u>Real</u> (and <u>Really</u> and <u>immediately</u> ego-Vanishing) approach to Truth must be made possible for all-and-All—by Means of My Avatarically Self-Transmitted (and Immediately ego-Vanishing) Divine Grace. And it is not necessary for any <u>one</u> to be qualified for <u>any</u> <u>other</u> approach to Truth—because My Avatarically Self-Transmitted (and Immediately ego-Vanishing) Divine Grace is (now, and forever hereafter) Freely Available to all-and-All. Therefore, My Avatarically Self-Transmitted (and Immediately ego-Vanishing) Divine Grace Is the Only Necessary Competence. And My Avatarically Self-Transmitted (and Immediately ego-Vanishing) Divine Grace cannot be either deserved or earned. My Avatarically Self-Transmitted (and Immediately ego-Vanishing) Divine Grace Is a Paradox, Mysteriously Given. Therefore, in order for you to Enjoy the Competence That My Avatarically Self-Transmitted Free Gift of Immediately ego-Vanishing Divine Grace Freely and Really Establishes in My any and every true devotee, it is only necessary that My Free Gift of My

Self-Evidently Divine Person (Which <u>Is</u> the Very Form, and Presence, and State Of Avatarically ego-Vanishing Divine Grace) be Honored by you, in heart-True devotional Acknowledgement of Me, and truly devotionally Me-recognizing and Really devotionally to-Me-responding devotional Reception of Me—and this (by Virtue of My Avatarically Self-Transmitted, and Immediately ego-Vanishing, Divine Grace Itself) to the degree (Most Ultimately) of devotionally Most Perfect Realization of Me.

"God"-Talk, Real-God-Realization, Most Perfect Divine Self-Awakening, and the Seven Possible Stages of Life

I.

There are only seven possible stages of life. And Real (Acausal) God (or Truth, or Reality) may (in any moment) be talked about from the (either real or imagined) "point of view" of any one of them. However, actual Real-God-Realization (or the Realization of Truth Itself, or Reality Itself) is profoundly more than talk (and thought), or even talking (and thinking) about talk. Indeed, the Way of Real-God-Realization (or the Way of the actual Realization of Truth Itself, or Reality Itself) truly begins where (and when) talk (and thinking) ceases.

II.

In the literature of Adidam,[12] Which is the Way That I have Revealed and Demonstrated for the sake of all-and-All, I have Described the seven potential stages of the progressive development of human life. Briefly, the seven stages of human life may be summarized as follows:

In the context of the first three stages of life, the gross body-mind complex is developed and coordinated. First, the gross physical is developed, then the emotional-sexual functions are developed and coordinated with the gross physical, and (finally) the mental functions and the function of the will are developed and coordinated with the emotional-sexual and gross physical functions. Optimally, all of this is nurtured, guided, and done in the context of love, trust, and surrender in relation to the Living Acausal Divine (or the all-and-All-Pervading and all-and-All-Transcending Real Acausal God, or Truth, or Reality).

In the context of the fourth stage of life, this now complex psycho-physical being is surrendered beyond itself, to and into the (all-and-All-Pervading, and all-and-All-Transcending, and Self-Evidently Divine) Source (or Source-Condition) That Pervades (and, yet, Transcends) it and the total world. This surrender is done to the point of conditional union with that Divine Source (or Source-Condition). In due course, such conditional union becomes, by Means of Divine Grace, conditional union with the Spiritual Presence (or Spirit-Current) of That Divine Source (or of That Divine Source-Condition, Truth, or Reality)—and this in occasions of experienced (descending) Bliss that involve and (simultaneously) transcend the body-mind.

In the context of the fifth stage of life, this process is continued, but the plane of conditional self-awareness ascends, to become dominantly subtle (or psychic), rather than gross (or merely physical)—and the Realization of conditional union with the (all-and-All-Pervading and all-and-All-Transcending) Divine Source (or Source-Condition) involves experiences of ascended attention that eventually go beyond physical references, and (at last) even beyond mental references.

In the context of the sixth stage of life, attention (which is the causal root, or base, of the mind) is inverted (or, by one or another means, surrendered), away from gross and subtle states and objects of the body-mind, and toward its own Root, even the Ultimate Root of the ego-self—Which is the Witness-Consciousness (when attention is active), and Which is also (Ultimately) Consciousness Itself (Prior to objects, and Prior to the sense of separate self). The Ultimate result of this exercise is conditional Realization of the Transcendental Self-Condition, or the intuition of Self-Existing Transcendental Being—which intuition remains strategically (and, otherwise, tacitly) dissociated from all objects (even if, as in the case of sixth stage "Sahaja Nirvikalpa Samadhi", the natural perception and conception of phenomenal objects is freely allowed).

In the only-by-Me Revealed and Given seventh stage of life, there is Prior and Non-conditional (or Inherent, and Inherently Most Perfect) Self-Identification with Self-Existing and Self-Radiant Transcendental (and Self-Evidently Divine) Being, or the Divine Conscious Light (Itself)—the Ultimate (Divine) Identity of all beings (or subjects), and the Ultimate (Divine) Self-Condition of all conditions (or objects). This Prior (or Inherent) and Inherently Most Perfect Self-Identification (or Divine Self-Abiding) is directly Realized (by Means of My Avataric Divine Spiritual Grace), entirely apart from any dissociative act of inversion. And, while Divinely Self-Abiding (Thus), if any conditions arise (or if any states of body-mind arise), they are simply (Divinely) Self-Recognized in the Self-Existing and Self-Radiant Condition of Being (as transparent, or merely apparent, and un-necessary, and inherently non-binding modifications of Itself). Such is seventh stage Sahaja Nirvikalpa Samadhi—and It is Inherently Free of any apparent implications, limitations, or binding power of phenomenal conditions. If no conditions arise to the notice, there is simply the Self-Existing and Self-Radiant Condition of Transcendental, Inherently Spiritual, Inherently egoless, and Self-Evidently Divine Being. Such is Absolute (or Inherently Most Perfect) Realization of That about Which nothing sufficient can be said—and there is not Anyone, Anything, or Anywhere beyond It to be Realized.

III.

Individuals (at one or another stage or moment) in the first six stages of life either pursue (but do not yet Most Perfectly Awaken to) the Realization of Real (Acausal) God (or of Truth Itself, or Reality Itself) or they (otherwise) submit to lesser purposes (relative to self-fulfillment at any particular stage of life) or (in the context of either the fourth or the fifth or the sixth stage of life, because of the characteristic limitations of the particular stage of life) they submit to one or another (conditionally achieved, conditionally determined, and conditionally limited) form of presumed "Real-God-Realization" that is dependent upon the (necessarily, conditional) exercise of the body, or the body-mind, or the mind, or (simply) attention itself. Therefore, strictly speaking, Real-God-Realization (or the Realization of Truth Itself, or Reality Itself) is a characteristic only of the (only-by-Me Revealed and Given) Final and Complete (or seventh) stage of life. However, less strictly speaking (or, as a matter of conventional reference, intended to honor the truly profound developmental demonstrations that may precede the only-by-My-Avataric-Divine-Spiritual-Grace-Given Realization of the seventh stage of life), the term "Real-God-Realization" (and the term "Real-God-Realizer") may also be applied to cases and degrees of developmental demonstration in the context of either the fourth, or the fifth, or the sixth stage of life.

IV.

The first three stages of life—not informed or inspired by the Wisdom of the fourth, the fifth, the sixth, or the seventh stage of life—are (in themselves) characterized by the pursuit of (body-based) self-fulfillment (even via self-indulgence, or else via socially established conventions of morality, self-discipline, and rather materialistic hope).

The fourth and the fifth stages of life (not informed or inspired by the Wisdom of either the sixth or the seventh stage of life) are (in themselves) characterized by the pursuit of "soul"-based (or, really, mind-based, or psyche-based) and natural-energy-based (or even Spirit-based) self-glorification— at first, via popular religious faith and practice, and, then, via every kind of (progressively) esoteric, and (possibly) Spiritual, and (otherwise) Yogic searching for "eternal life" (or immortality), whether of body _and_ "soul" or (otherwise) simply of "soul".

The sixth stage of life (which is the last of the egoic, or ego-based and psycho-physically determined, stages of life) is characterized by one or more of three possible persuasions (and efforts), each (to one or another degree) yet influenced (or limited) by the fundamental presumption of the first five stages of life. And each of these three persuasions (and efforts), even (potentially) following on one another (progressively), pursues (or, at last, Affirms) Freedom from the body-mind (or the conditional self in the context of the "Cosmic Round" and the first five stages of life), by means of a particular mode of strategic dissociation from the body-mind.

And only the (only-by-Me-Revealed and Given) seventh stage of life is characterized (inherently, and by progressive stages of Demonstration[13]) by Non-conditional (or Most Perfect) Real-God-Realization _Itself_ (or the Absolute, or Most Perfect, Realization of Truth Itself, or Inherently Perfect Reality Itself), Utterly and Inherently (and Inherently Most Perfectly) Transcending egoity (or self-bondage, separateness, and "difference") itself.

V.

The first three stages of life are, from the "point of view" associated with any of the stages of life beyond them, the stages of "gross ignorance" (or the ordinary stages of progressive functional self-development, in themselves bereft of any Influence or Wisdom greater than material Nature).

From the "point of view" of any of the three orientations that are potential in the context of the sixth stage of life, the fourth and the fifth stages of life are the stages of "subtle ignorance" (or the stages of seeking toward the inherently impossible Goal of an eternal—or permanent, unopposed, and only Happy—<u>conditional</u> state and <u>conditional</u> circumstance of self-perfection and self-fulfillment).

And, from the "Point of View" of the (only-by-Me Revealed and Given) seventh stage of life, even the sixth stage of life is limited by the basic Illusion (or by the basic apparent problem)—or (at least) by strategic attention to the basic Illusion (or to the basic apparent problem)—of a separate self (or of a substantively, rather than merely apparently, separate self-essence, or even an essential and eternal, or substantively permanent and unchanging, ego-"I"). Thus, from the "Point of View" of the (only-by-Me Revealed and Given) seventh stage of life, the sixth stage of life is limited by "causal ignorance" (or the <u>essence</u> of ignorance)—until (in the potential real transition to the only-by-Me Revealed and Given seventh stage of life) <u>only</u> the Non-conditional (or Perfectly Subjective) Absolute (or Real Acausal God, or Truth, or Reality) <u>Itself</u> is Non-conditionally (and Inherently Most Perfectly) Realized As the Obvious.

VI.

In the common world (of body-based and socially communicated conventions of aspiration and action), there is always a struggle in evidence—between the tendency of humankind to remain in "gross ignorance" (characterized by a materialistic culture of ego-satisfactions) and the necessity for humankind (one by one) to Grow Beyond the first three stages of life (by the Influence of Wisdom, at least beginning with the "faith-Principle" associated with the earliest dimension of the fourth stage of life). However, from the (only-by-Me Revealed and Given) Divine "Point of View" (of Truth Itself, or Reality Itself), there is always an even greater necessity (inherently Urged upon all)—which is for humankind (one by one) to Grow Beyond even all of the first six (or ego-based) stages of life, to Most Perfectly Realize the (Truly Ultimate and Inherent) Freedom of Absolute Being (Self-Existing, As Consciousness Itself, and Self-Radiant, As Love-Bliss Itself).

VII.

The ultimate (or final) stage of egoity (and of ego-transcendence) is the sixth stage of life. Therefore, rightly understood, the first five stages of life are (in the context of the Great Tradition) a process of Growth (of progressive psycho-physical self-awareness)—until the "point of view" of the sixth stage of life is truly (and stably) Realized.

When the "point of view" of "gross ignorance" (and the pursuit of gross self-indulgence and gross, or body-based, self-fulfillment) ceases to be the limit of individual awareness, the "point of view" of "subtle ignorance" (and the pursuit of subtle self-eternalization) begins (and develops progressively). At any time after that new beginning—or, at the earliest, once the gross bodily "point of view" has been thoroughly released by submission to the subtle (or psyche-based, and natural-energy-based), or even (possibly) Spirit-based, "point of view"—the "point of view" of the root-self (prior to "Nature", prior to body and mind, and, therefore, also prior to psyche, or "soul") may be Realized, thus releasing even the subtle (or psyche-based and natural-energy-based) "point of view" itself, and activating the potential (even, possibly, in Spiritual terms) of the sixth stage of life.

And the sixth stage of life (which is the ultimate effort to achieve ego-transcendence) is a course that is (or may be) progressively associated with one or more of three principal orientations (in practice): either asceticism (or the extreme orientation toward annihilation of the psycho-physical self), or the more moderately self-disciplined course and orientation toward pacification of the psycho-physical self, or the ultimate course and orientation toward Non-conditional (or Perfectly Subjective) Self-Identification (and tacit, or effortless, transcending of the psycho-physical self).

VIII.

I n the Great Tradition (or common Wisdom-Inheritance)
of humankind, the characteristic (or grossly ignorant)
orientation of the first three stages of life (in themselves,
or engaged for their own sake) is always everywhere dis-
played in the common world (to date), and every age (or
epoch) displays its own unique convention (or style) of
materialistic purposiveness.

In the Great Tradition of humankind, the characteristic
orientation of the fourth and fifth stages of life is found (first
of all) in the traditional popular religions (such as Hinduism,
Christianity, Islam, and Judaism), and in all the esoteric
traditions of fourth and fifth stage religious mysticism and
mystical Spirituality (or descending and ascending Yoga).

In the Great Tradition of humankind, the characteristic
orientation of the sixth stage of life is found in its first (or
ascetical) form in such traditions as Samkhya and Jainism,
and in its second (or moderate and self-pacifying, or "Middle
Way") form principally in the traditions (or schools) of
Buddhism (and also in the schools of Taoism), and in its third
(or final, and Non-conditionally, or Perfectly Subjectively,
Self-Affirming) form principally in the traditions (or schools)
of Advaitism (or "Non-Dualism"), especially that of Advaita
Vedanta (and, secondarily, or with less directness, within the
schools of some varieties of Buddhism, especially within the
"Mahayana" and "Vajrayana" traditions, and also, but with
even less directness, within some schools of Taoism).

In the Great Tradition of humankind (previous to My
Avataric Divine Appearance here), the characteristic (or
Divinely, or Most Perfectly, Enlightened) "Orientation" (or
"Point of View") of the seventh stage of life has not been
Realized and Demonstrated. There has been occasional
seeming (or suggestive) evidence, in the Teachings of a
random few unique individuals and traditions—especially

within the schools of Advaitism, and, secondarily (or by a less direct and characteristic expression) within some schools of Buddhism, and (but with an even less direct and characteristic expression) within some schools of Taoism—of limited foreshadowings (or partial intuitions, or insightful, but limited, premonitions) of the characteristic (or Divinely, or Most Perfectly, Enlightened) "Orientation" (or "Point of View") of the seventh stage of life—but that evidence is only verbal, or limited to expressions of a philosophical persuasion only, and a philosophical persuasion that is (itself) founded on the sixth stage orientation, practice, and possible Realization that preceded (and still limits, in every case) the apparently "seventh stage" expression or Teaching.

IX.

I Am Adi Da Samraj—the Adi-Guru, the Ati-Guru, the Original and Eternal Teacher, the Divine World-Teacher, here to Complete the Great Tradition of humankind. I Am the Ruchira Avatar, the Da Avatar, the Love-Ananda Avatar, the Tathagata Avatar, the Ruchira Buddha, the Purushottama Buddha, the Ashvamedha Buddha, the Adi-Buddha Avatar, the Ati-Buddha Avatar, the Ruchira Siddha,[14] the All-Completing Adept, the First, Last, and Only Avataric Divine Adept-Revealer (or Siddha) of the seventh stage of life. I Am the seventh stage Avataric Divine Realizer, Avataric Divine Revealer, and Avataric Divine Self-Revelation of Real (Acausal) God, Truth, and Reality—Given in this "late-time" (or would-be Complete and potentially Consummate era) and in this now "dark" epoch (as it must be described from the Realized Divine and Spiritual "Point of View", and with regard to the tendencies of the times),[15] and Given for the sake of Completion (of the progressive human Ordeal) and for the sake of Unity (or the cooperative re-Union of humankind).

By Means of My Avatarically Full-Given Divine Word, I have Revealed the characteristic and the (to one degree or another, and in one manner or another) always limited design and the (to one degree or another, and in one manner or another) always ego-based nature of each and all of the first six stages of life (in and of themselves). And, by Means of My Avatarically Full-Given Divine Word, I have Revealed the Unique Avataric Divine Transcendental Spiritual Way of Adidam (or Adidam Ruchiradam)—Which is also called (by Me) "The Way of Is" (or "The Transcendental Spiritual Way of Is"), and "The Way of Reality Itself" (or "The Transcendental Spiritual Way of Reality Itself"), and "The Way of Conscious Light" (or "The Transcendental Spiritual Way of Conscious Light"), and "The Universal Transcendental Spiritual Way of 'Sri Hridayam'" (or "The Transcendental Spiritual Way of the True Divine Heart", or "The 'Radical' Way of the Heart Itself", or, simply, "The 'Radical' Way of the

Heart"), and "The Way of 'Perfect Knowledge'" (or "The Transcendental Spiritual Way of 'Perfect Knowledge'"), and "The Way of 'Radical' self-Understanding" (or "The Transcendental Spiritual Way of 'Radical' self-Understanding", or "The Transcendental Spiritual Way of 'Radical' ego-Transcendence"), and "The Way of 'Radical' Devotional Knowledge" (or "The Transcendental Spiritual Way of 'Radical' Devotional Knowledge"), and "The Way of Divine Ignorance" (or "The Transcendental Spiritual Way of Divine Ignorance", or "The Transcendental Spiritual Way of Positive Disillusionment"), and "The Transcendental Spiritual Way of 'Radical' Non-Dualism" (or "Ruchira Avatara Advaita-Dharma", or "Ruchira Advaitism", or "Ruchira Buddhism", or "Advaitayana Buddhism", or "Buddhayana Advaitism", or "Hridaya-Advaita Dharma"), and "The Transcendental Way of Divine Spiritual Baptism" (or "Ruchira Avatara Siddha Yoga", or "Ruchira Siddha Yoga", or "Ruchira Avatara Shaktipat Yoga", or "Ruchira Shaktipat Yoga", or "Ruchira Avatara Hridaya-Siddha Yoga", or "Ruchira Avatara Hridaya-Shaktipat Yoga", or "Ruchira Avatara Maha-Jnana-Siddha Yoga", or "Ruchira Avatara Maha-Jnana Hridaya-Shaktipat Yoga")[16]—in Which the ego is directly and effectively transcended in the context of each and all of the first six stages of life (so that the seventh stage of life may be Realized). Likewise, by Means of My Avatarically Full-Given Divine Word, I have Revealed every Characteristic, Sign, Design, and Process associated with the Realization and the Demonstration of the (Inherently, and Inherently Most Perfectly, egoless) seventh (and Final) stage of life. By Means of My Avatarically Full-Given Divine Work of Demonstration and Blessing, I have Revealed the seventh stage of life in and by and As My Own Avatarically-Born bodily (human) Divine Form and Life. And I have altogether Fulfilled My Avataric Divine Revelation-Purpose by Accomplishing (through the Universally both Given and Demonstrated Divine Siddhis of My all-and-All-Blessing Avataric Divine Work) the Firm Establishment of That Which Is Necessary for the eventual seventh stage

Realization and (Finally, or Most Ultimately) Divine Translation of even all conditionally manifested beings.

The Great Tradition of humankind (previous to My Avataric Divine Appearance here) must generally be understood only in the (necessarily, limited) terms of the first six stages of life. Whenever (even previous to My Avataric Divine Appearance here) the sixth stage of life has been entered, the seventh stage of life has been, in principle, also the potential of human Realization. However, the seventh stage Adept-Revelation was not then Given (and It is only now Given, by Me), and the Divine Secrets of true ego-transcendence and of the Divine Yoga of the Most Ultimate (or seventh stage) Demonstration were not then Given (and They are only now Given, by Me). The (always potential) seventh stage Realization and Demonstration did not Appear until I Appeared, in order to Fully Reveal and to Fully Demonstrate the seventh stage of life and, by the Very Act of My Fullest Avataric Divine Appearance here and everywhere (and by Means of all My Unique Avataric Divine Siddha-Work of Adept-Service here and everywhere), to make the seventh stage Realization and Demonstration possible for all who heart-respond to Me, and who practice (ego-surrendering, ego-forgetting, and, more and more, ego-transcending) devotion to Me, and who (altogether, and firmly) embrace and practice the only-by-Me Revealed and Given Way of Adidam.[17] Therefore, relative to the seventh stage of life, the Great Tradition of humankind (previous to My Avataric Divine Appearance here) produced only limited foreshadowings (or partial intuitions, or insightful, but limited, premonitions), in the form of a few, random philosophical expressions that appear in the midst of the traditional sixth stage literatures.[18] And it is these few and yet limited traditional expressions that must be studied in order to understand the character and the degree of humankind's exploration of the possibility of the seventh stage of life previous to the (now and forever) future time of My Fully Real-God-Revealing, Truth-Revealing, and Reality-Revealing Work and Word.

X.

There are (basically) only five possible orientations (or "points of view"), each built upon (or OutGrowing, or transcending) the one immediately previous to itself.

The first (or the least) of these may be called "Conventional Monism". According to this "point of view", the world (or cosmic Nature) is all there is, and it is a material Unity, also expressed as the individual body-mind (which is itself a material unity). And this "point of view" accounts for all lesser or gross (or materialistic, body-based, and, necessarily, mortal) orientations or searches in the (always struggling, and never truly, or finally, fulfilled) context of the first three stages of life in the human domain.

The second (or next) possible orientation (or "point of view") may be called "Conventional Dualism". According to this "point of view", the world (or even the Totality of Existence) is made up of a number of principal pairs (whether simply natural or, somehow otherwise, hierarchical). Most typically, the first of these principal pairs is the hierarchically conceived pair of "God" and the world—with "God" sometimes called (and, otherwise, commonly, and even popularly, conceived as) "Purushottama", combining both "Purusha" (or "Being" and "Consciousness") and "Prakriti" (meaning, in this conception, "Creativity" and "Creative Energy", or "Creator-Energy"). And the other principal (and, most typically, hierarchically conceived) pairs include "God" and the "soul" (or the psyche, or the subtle personality), and also the "soul" and the world, and also the mind (or the psyche, or the "soul") and the body. Each half of each hierarchically conceived pair (or even each natural pair) is (according to this "point of view") related to (and interrelated with) the other half of the pair, but (paradoxically, and especially in the case of hierarchically conceived pairs) each half of each pair is also utterly "different" than (or even inherently separate from) the other half of the pair. And the obligatory "Goal" of each presumed lesser (or dependent) half of each hierarchically related pair is to submit to (and, eventually, even to ascend to) the greater (or higher) half of the pair. Therefore, from this "point of view", the "soul" (and even the total world) must submit to (and, eventually, ascend to) "God" (or "God"-Realization). Likewise, the body must submit (or be submitted) to the mind (or the psyche, or the "soul"). Indeed, all that which (in the human being) is "of the world" must, according to the hierarchical conception, submit (or be submitted) to (and, in turn, be relinquished by) the "soul", which must itself (in turn, and by submitting to "God", and to the Urge to "God"-Realization) eventually and progressively ascend to "God". And this total Process is, indeed, the total Process characteristically (and traditionally) associated with the fourth and the fifth stages of life, and such great fourth and fifth stage popular (or exoteric, and, otherwise, esoteric) traditions as have appeared in (or among) the forms of Hinduism, Christianity, Islam, and Judaism, and (in their own unique manner) in (or among) the forms of Taoism, and (also uniquely) even in (or among) some forms of Buddhism.

The third (and next) possible orientation (or "point of view") may be called "Primary Dualism". According to this "point of view", the Totality of Existence is an apparent combination of only two Primary Realities. These Primary Realities are traditionally called "Purusha" (or Non-conditional, and, As Such, Inherently Perfect, and Perfectly and Necessarily Subjective, "Being" and "Consciousness") and "Prakriti" (or "Objective Energy", Which, modified, appears as the body, the mind, all objects, and all others). From this "point of view", this "Primary Duality" must, first of all, be understood (by observation and intuition) to be actual (or Really So). Then Purusha (or the conscious self, which—according to the characteristic, and paradoxical, traditional "point of view" of "Primary Dualism"—Is, Ultimately, a Perfectly Subjective, or Non-conditional, but also specific, independent, and individual, Self) must separate itself (basically, by willful ascetical discipline) from Prakriti (or the body, the mind, all their objects, and all others). And this "point of view" and Process (which seeks to be released from the body-mind, or from the illusory need to eternalize the body, the mind, or the body-mind) is the first possible "point of view" and Process traditionally associated with the sixth stage of life (and such great sixth stage traditions as have appeared within Jainism, and the ancient philosophical tradition of Samkhya).

The fourth (and next to last) possible orientation (or "point of view") may be called "Secondary Non-Dualism" (or "Secondary Absolute Monism"). According to this "point of view", there is no inherently independent and separate (or separable) Purusha (either as an eternal, and Non-conditional, individual Self or, according to some proponents, As Absolute Being Itself, or Absolute Consciousness Itself), but the Totality of Existence is only Prakriti (conditionally appearing as a beginningless and endless continuum of causes and effects, or, in effect, modifications of Prakriti, or of "Energy Itself"). Therefore, according to this "point of view", Prakriti (or "Energy Itself") appears (and must be so observed) only as ephemeral (and observable, or objective) changes, preceded and followed by equally ephemeral (and equally observable, or objective) changes, until (by the Process of observation, insight, and self-pacification) the Inherent (or Original, or Nirvanic) State of Prakriti (or of "Energy Itself") is Realized. (However, there is an Ultimate Paradox necessarily associated with this orientation, or "point of view", and Process—for, if the Realization of the Original, or Nirvanic, State of Prakriti, or of "Energy Itself", is, in fact, achieved, how can That Realization be differentiated from—

or, otherwise, be presumed to Be other than, or not Identical to—Absolute Consciousness Itself?) In any case, this "point of view" and Process (which seeks to be released from both the illusory need to eternalize the conditional self and the equally illusory need to annihilate the conditional self—and which "point of view" and Process may, therefore, follow upon, or, otherwise, supersede, the "point of view" and Process of "Primary Dualism") is the second possible "point of view" and Process traditionally associated with the sixth stage of life (and such great sixth stage schools as have appeared within the traditions of Buddhism, and also within the tradition of Taoism).

The fifth (and final) possible orientation (or "point of view") may be called "Ultimate Non-Dualism" (or "Primary Absolute Monism"). According to this "point of view", there is (in Truth) no Prakriti (or separate and independent "Objective Energy", or any separate and independent body, mind, object, or other at all), but the Totality of Existence is only the One and Absolute Purusha (or Self-Existing and Self-Radiant Consciousness Itself). From this "point of view", this "Ultimate Absolute" (or this Non-conditional—and, As Such, Inherently Perfect, and Perfectly Subjective—Reality) must, first of all, be understood (and directly intuited) to be actual (or Really So), and then Perfectly (or Utterly) Affirmed (By direct Self-Identification with Consciousness Itself). This "point of view" and Process (which may follow upon, or be "Uncovered" by, the "point of view" and Process of "Secondary Non-Dualism", and which may even immediately follow upon, or be "Uncovered" by, the "point of view" and Process of "Primary Dualism") is the third (and final, and Principal) possible "point of view" and Process traditionally (and inherently) associated with the sixth stage of life (and such great sixth stage schools as have appeared in the form of the traditions of Advaitism, and also, secondarily, or with less directness, within the schools of some varieties of Buddhism, especially within the Mahayana and Vajrayana traditions, and, but with even less directness, within some of the schools of Taoism).

Most Ultimately, this "point of view" and Process (of "Ultimate Non-Dualism", or "Primary Absolute Monism") is (if it is, by Means Of My Avatarically Self-Transmitted Divine Spiritual Grace, Most Perfectly Realized) the "Point of View" (and the Most Perfect Process) that (by all the Graceful Means I have Revealed and Given for the sake of all who will be My devotees) establishes and characterizes the seventh stage of life. And, because (from the thoroughly Non-Dualistic "Point of View" that necessarily characterizes the seventh stage of life) the "Ultimate Absolute" Is both Self-Existing (As Absolute Being Itself and Absolute Consciousness Itself) and Self-Radiant (As Absolute, and Perfectly Subjective, Spiritual Energy, Love-Bliss-Energy, Itself), It (or That One) could (as well as by many other possible, and even traditional, terms) be rightly indicated interchangeably by either the traditional term "Purusha" (intended in the Absolute, All-Inclusive, or Non-Exclusive, and Non-Dualistic sense) or the (likewise intended) traditional term "Maha-Purusha" (meaning "Great Purusha", or "Supreme Purusha") or the (likewise intended) traditional term "Purushottama" (also meaning "Supreme Purusha"), indicating (in each case) the One, Absolute, and Non-Separate (or Inherently All-Inclusive, or Perfectly Non-Exclusive) Real (Acausal) God, or Truth, or Reality.

XI.

Even though the schools of "Primary Dualism" (such as are to be found within the traditions of Samkhya and Jainism) contain (by virtue of the very presumption of "Dualism") at least a tendency toward practices (and/or experiences) associated with the ascent of the "soul", the primary language of all traditions of "Primary Dualism" suggests not only the utter relinquishment of all physical, psycho-physical, and psychic conditions and states, but also the utter relinquishment of all physical, psycho-physical, and psychic means. Indeed, the sixth stage Ultimate Goal (or Result) of "Primary Dualism" is the same as That of "Secondary Non-Dualism" and "Ultimate Non-Dualism". However, the philosophy and practice associated with the schools of "Primary Dualism" (principally within the traditions of Samkhya and Jainism) are built upon an analysis of existence as experienced from the gross (or bodily) "point of view". Therefore, the "method" of "Primary Dualism" is primarily ascetical (or a bodily intensive effort to relinquish, or to release the Deep Being from, body-consciousness and all psycho-physical states).

The sixth stage Ultimate Goal (or Result) of "Secondary Non-Dualism" is the same as That of "Primary Dualism" and "Ultimate Non-Dualism". However, the philosophy and practice associated with the schools of "Secondary Non-Dualism", principally within the traditions of Buddhism (and also within the tradition of Taoism), are built upon an analysis of existence as experienced from the subtle (or mental, or even energy-essence) "point of view". Therefore, the Buddhist "method" of "Secondary Non-Dualism" is primarily associated with mental disciplines (originally classified under the heading of the discipline of "mindfulness", or simple observation and comprehension of psycho-physical states, and later extended in the form of a wide variety of religious, philosophical, and Yogic techniques), and (by this "method") the Buddhist form of "Secondary Non-Dualism" seeks to pacify the total body-mind (and, thus and thereby, to relinquish, or be released from, the <u>idea</u> of separate and independent self). Similarly, although the Taoist "method" of "Secondary Non-Dualism" is primarily associated with disciplines of natural energy (or disciplines of body and mind in relation to pervasive natural energy), rather than sheerly (or primarily) mental disciplines (or even mind-energy disciplines), the Taoist "method" of "Secondary Non-Dualism" also pursues a general pacification of the total body-mind. Thus, in whatever tradition it may appear, the "method" of "Secondary Non-Dualism" seeks and achieves detachment and release from the body-mind through a process of general psycho-physical pacification, whereas the "method" of "Primary Dualism" seeks and achieves detachment and release from the body-mind through an intense ascetical effort (often characterized by excessive bodily self-denial).

The "method" of "Ultimate Non-Dualism" is a matter of direct (or Non-conditional) Self-Identification with That Which Is the generally intended (sixth stage) Goal of both "Primary Dualism" and "Secondary Non-Dualism". That is to say, the philosophy and practice associated with the schools of "Ultimate Non-Dualism", principally in the traditions of Advaitism (and, secondarily, or with less directness, in some schools of Buddhism, and, with even less directness, in some schools of Taoism), are built upon (or developed from) an analysis (or a direct comprehension) of existence as "experienced" (or, rather, "Witnessed") from the "Point of View" of Consciousness Itself (rather than the "point of view" of either the body or the mind)—and the "method" of "Ultimate Non-Dualism" is that of Standing (tacitly and effortlessly) <u>As</u> Consciousness Itself (or the Ultimate, and Perfectly, or Nonconditionally, Subjective Reality Itself), Which Is <u>Inherently</u> Free of identification with the body-mind (and, therefore,

Priorly Released from identification with, or bondage to and by, the body-mind). Thus, the "method" of "Ultimate Non-Dualism" is one of <u>direct</u> (or Perfectly Subjective) Self-Identification with (or Self-Abiding <u>As</u>) That Which Is (otherwise) only the generally intended (sixth stage) Goal of the ascetical conditional efforts of "Primary Dualism" and the self-pacifying conditional efforts of "Secondary Non-Dualism".

The "Self-Abiding" discipline of "Ultimate Non-Dualism" also achieves the renunciation of body and mind, but by the most direct Means of (Perfectly Subjective) Self-Abiding, whereas "Primary Dualism" and "Secondary Non-Dualism" both seek "Ultimate Non-Duality" by the conditional means of either asceticism or self-pacification. However, it is also generally the case (in actual practice) that the Real Process of Self-Abiding (or direct and profound Self-Identification with Consciousness Itself, Prior to body and mind) begins (or develops) only after (or in the course of) degrees of practice (previous to the sixth stage of life, or, otherwise, in the context of the sixth stage of life) wherein either ascetical or self-pacifying disciplines (or both, with ascetical disciplines usually becoming progressively replaced by the more self-pacifying approach) are engaged until identification with the body and the mind is sufficiently released to stably allow the direct approach of Non-conditional Self-Identification with Consciousness Itself.

In the context of the sixth stage of life, the "point of view" and Process of "Primary Dualism" may or may not <u>fully</u> appear, but it invariably appears (in the context of the sixth stage of life, or earlier) as a <u>tendency</u> (in mind and body) toward excessive self-discipline (or extreme and fruitless asceticism). Therefore, if this tendency appears, it must eventually be understood—and it must then be replaced by a more moderate tendency toward self-discipline (or self-renunciation), which may or may not itself <u>fully</u> appear (in the context of the sixth stage of life) as the orientation of

"Secondary Non-Dualism", but which is (nonetheless) characterized (at any stage of life) by a motive toward self-transcendence (or Real ego-transcendence) that (in itself) would achieve a state of utter self-purification (or utter self-pacification).

Utter self-purification (or utter self-pacification) is not possible, and (in any case) it is not (itself) Real-God-Realization (or the Realization of Truth Itself, or Reality Itself). Therefore, if the only-by-Me Revealed and Given seventh stage of life is to be Realized, the limits of (or the search associated with) the moderate (and necessary) orientation toward self-renunciation must eventually be understood, and even the motive of self-renunciation must then (in the context of the sixth stage of life) be itself transcended, simply and most directly, through Prior Self-Identification with the Inherently Perfect and Perfectly Subjective (and Self-Evidently Divine), Non-Dual (or Absolute), Self-Existing, and Self-Radiant Truth (or Reality Itself)— Which Is Existence (or Being) Itself, Consciousness Itself, and Happiness (or Love-Bliss) Itself. And, in the Ultimate course of this Ultimate Process, Final and Complete (or seventh stage) Real-God-Realization Itself (or the Unqualified, or Absolute, or Inherently Most Perfect, Realization of Truth Itself, or Inherently Perfect Reality Itself) becomes Perfectly possible (by Means Of My Avatarically Self-Transmitted Divine Spiritual Grace).

XII.

The word "religion" has traditionally been understood as meaning "to bind again" (or "to rejoin", or "to make, or, otherwise, affirm, the Great Union", or, Ultimately, "to Realize That Condition Which Is Inherently and Only and Perfectly One, and Not Two").

Common (or exoteric, or conventional) religion (most of which is confined to aspirations and activities in the context of the first three stages of life) largely consists of ritualized magic, political and moral imperatives, and myths that idealize the "good" man and the "good" woman. And by such common (or exoteric, or conventional) religion, human beings may (it is hoped) be effectively oriented, by everyday cultural means, toward behaviors that positively address and serve the personal and collective material survival potentiality of their body-based humanity. However, strictly speaking, true religion (or religion that is, by definition, true, or faithful, to the profound and now and anciently honored sacred Process of the progressive, and would-be Most Perfect, Realization of That Condition Which Is, Itself, Inherently and Only and Perfectly One) is the (traditionally, rather esoteric) Process of progress toward actual Real-God-Realization (or toward the actual Realization of Acausal Truth Itself, or Acausal Reality Itself). Therefore, strictly speaking, true (and, traditionally, rather esoteric) religion (or religion that is truly effective Godwardly, or toward Acausal Truth Itself, or Acausal Reality Itself) truly begins no earlier than when "Conventional (or materialistic and body-based) Monism" is (at least beginning to be) replaced by "Conventional (or eternalistic and psyche-based) Dualism".

The principal exoteric religious idea is that all things and beings are in (and of) a Unity.

Therefore, the principal practice of exoteric religion (or religion in the general context of the first three stages of life) is the ritual (and otherwise magical, or even scientific) and also ethical (or social-moral) affirmation and (it is hoped) demonstration of the Universal (and even material) Unity.

The principal esoteric religious idea is that all things and beings are only mind (or a psychic phenomenon, or, merely, a psychic Illusion).

Therefore, the practice of esoteric religion is a matter of either the practice of intentional exploitation of mind (toward its higher development) or the practice whereby the mind itself is (directly and effectively) transcended.

The lesser response to the principal esoteric religious idea is the religious activity (characteristic of the fourth and the fifth stages of life) which seeks to develop the mind (and, thus, the conditional self and the conditional world, or worlds).

The greater (or Ultimate) response to the principal esoteric religious idea is the religious activity (characteristic of the sixth stage of life, and of the only-by-Me Revealed and Given seventh stage of life) which directly and effectively transcends the mind (and, thus, the Illusion of conditional self and conditional world, or worlds).

And, as I have now and fully Revealed and Demonstrated to all, the Most Ultimate Purpose of religion is Fulfilled only when all possible aspects of the preliminary course of religion (or all aspects of the first six stages of life) are (by Means of My Avataric Divine Spiritual Grace) transcended in the fullest (Final and Complete and Inherently Most Perfect, or only-by-Me Revealed and Given seventh stage) Realization of That "Ultimate Non-Duality" Which Is Real (Acausal) God, or Acausal Truth Itself, or Acausal Reality Itself, and Which Is One and Perfection Itself.

So Be It.

XIII.

From the "point of view" of the gross body (or gross conditional existence), everything (including mind and Consciousness) is perceived, conceived, and presumed to be an irreducibly material, finite, mortal process.

From the "point of view" of the mind (or subtle conditional existence), everything (including the gross body and all gross conditions) is perceived, conceived, and presumed to be an effect—made of the Infinite Objective "Substance" (or the Infinite Cosmic Reservoir) of Indestructible (and, Ultimately, Indivisible) Cosmic Light (or Cosmic Mind Itself), and caused by (and within) the Infinite Totality of Cosmic Mind. And even the Totality of Cosmic Mind (including the individual mind, and Consciousness Itself) is, thus, presumed to be Cosmic Light Itself (or not other than Cosmic Mind Itself).

From the "Point of View" of Consciousness Itself, everything conditional, objective, or objectified (whether gross or subtle or causal in nature) is perceived, conceived, and presumed to <u>Be</u> Consciousness Itself (or the Ultimate and Transcendental and Inherently Spiritual, or Love-Blissful, and Perfectly Subjective Reality Itself), such that conditional, objective, or objectified reality is Inherently Realized to be a merely apparent modification (or an illusory "play") of, in, and upon the Native Radiance (or Intrinsic Self-Radiance) of Consciousness Itself.

These three primary perceptions, conceptions, or presumptions also correspond (variously) to the seven potential stages of life.

The perception, conception, or presumption based on the "point of view" of gross conditional existence corresponds to the conventional perception, conception, or presumption associated with the first three stages of life. (And the cultural and general social bias toward "scientism", or "scientific materialism", or the gross-body-bound mentality that seeks, by means of gross-body-based "knowing", to achieve power, or manipulative advantage, over the natural world—and which tends, and even seeks, to bind or limit humankind to gross conditional nature, and to the even ancient tradition and philosophy of gross materialism—exemplifies this lower, or mundane, or adolescent orientation.)

The fourth stage of life is a transitional stage (or process)—originally grounded in (or naturally associated with) the gross conditional "point of view" of the first three stages of life, but Awakening (progressively) toward the (potential) "point of view", the perception, the conception, and the presumption of subtle conditional existence, mind (or total Cosmic Mind), and Cosmic Light. (And the process associated with the transition to, and through, the fourth stage of life is the source of popular "creationist", or "Creator-God", religions, as well as the popular, or less developed, forms of sainthood.)

The perception, conception, or presumption based on the "point of view" of subtle conditional existence, mind, and Cosmic Light (in Itself), or Cosmic Mind (in Itself), corresponds to the perception, conception, or presumption associated with the fifth stage of life. (And the conceptions and practices associated with the fifth stage of life are the primary traditional sources of all that is commonly known as higher esoteric, or secret and higher and mystical, religion and Spirituality.)

The perception, conception, or presumption based on the object-excluding "Point of View" of Consciousness Itself corresponds to the perception, conception, or presumption associated with the sixth stage of life. (And the sixth stage of life is the basic, or common, source of Transcendentalist conceptions and traditions of Enlightenment, or Liberation.)

Any one of the three primary modes of perception, conception, or presumption I have just Described could be (and is) affirmed by individuals, groups, and traditions in the human sphere—but which one of the three modes is ultimately correct (or expressive of Truth Itself)? It is the third—or the perception, conception, or presumption based on the "Point of View" of Consciousness Itself. Why? Because, no matter what arises as your experience or knowledge (whether gross or subtle or causal, and whether of body or of mind), you <u>Are</u> the Witness of it—and That Which <u>Is</u> the Witness <u>Is</u> Consciousness Itself.

No matter what arises, you <u>Are</u> Consciousness Itself. You are never really (or in Truth) separately identical to (or even Really, or in Truth, limited by) what is apparently objective (or functionally objectified) to you—but you tend to feel (or presume) specific (or separate) identification with (or, otherwise, limitation by) objective (or objectified) conditions, until you are able to inspect (and to be Inherently, and Inherently Perfectly, Identified with) your <u>Real</u> (or Native, or Inherent, and Inherently Perfect) "Situation", Which Is Always Already Free (or Acausally Self-Existing) Consciousness Itself, the Inherently Free "Subject" (or Perfectly Subjective Being) in the (apparent) context of conditional objects (or of apparently objectified Light), and Who (it must be Realized) Is the Acausally Self-Existing, Acausally Self-Radiant, and Self-Evidently Divine Self-Condition (or Being, or Person) of the One and Only and Inherently Indivisible and Inherently egoless Conscious Light That Is Always Already Prior to all conditional objects and Always Already Prior to apparently objectified Light (or apparently objectified Spirit-Energy) Itself. Therefore, the "points of view" of body and mind (and their perceptions, conceptions, or presumptions) are secondary to (and utterly dependent upon) the "Point of View" of Consciousness Itself (and the perception, conception, or presumption associated with Consciousness Itself).

The perceptions, conceptions, or presumptions based on the "points of view" of body and mind could not even be made, were body and mind not Always Already Founded in (or apparently Witnessed by) Consciousness Itself. Therefore, the perception, conception, or presumption based on the "Point of View" of Consciousness Itself is, also (beyond the object-excluding limitations of the sixth stage of life), the Root-Essence of the Divine Self-Realization of Reality (Itself) That Is the Very Basis and Context of the only-by-Me Revealed and Given seventh stage of life. When (in the Divine Self-Awakening to the only-by-Me Revealed and Given seventh stage of life) the body-mind and the conditional worlds are finally (Divinely) Self-Recognized to be transparent (or merely apparent), and un-necessary, and inherently non-binding modifications of the (by-Me-Avatarically-Self-Revealed) Transcendental, Inherently Spiritual, Inherently egoless, and Self-Evidently Divine Self-Condition (and Source-Condition), Then There Is Only Me, Only the "you" that is (Non-Separately, Beyond the ego-"I") not "different" from Me As I Am, Only One Self, Only Real (Acausal) God, Only Truth, Only Reality, Only Inherently egoless and Spiritually "Bright" Consciousness, Only Divine Love-Bliss, Only the Perfectly Subjective (and Tacit) Self-Apprehension of Being (Itself)—Only the One and Only and Inherently Indivisible and Inherently egoless Conscious Light That Is (even As all-and-All) and That Is Always Already (Perfectly Prior to all-and-All).

XIV.

The first five stages of life correspond to the conditionally apparent <u>psycho-physical</u> manifestations of the gross and the subtle structures and functions of the body-mind. The sixth stage of life corresponds to the conditionally apparent root of the gross and the subtle psycho-physical structures and functions—which conditionally apparent root is the causal structure and function of the body-mind. The only-by-Me Revealed and Given "Perfect Practice" of "Perfect Knowledge" involves a Disposition that Inherently Transcends the strategic exercise of the gross and the subtle and the causal structures and functions of conditionally apparent existence as a body-mind-self. Thus, in the only-by-Me Revealed and Given Way of Adidam, the "Perfect Practice" of "Perfect Knowledge" Inherently Transcends even the causal "body" (or the causal dimension of structure and function), without otherwise (in the sixth stage manner) strategically excluding (or dissociating from) the body-mind and the world.

The foundation of fifth stage traditions is the subtle "body" (or the subtle dimension of structure and function), and the (generally, esoteric) process of Yoga with reference to the psycho-physical context of the rather complex domain that is the subtle body (and, also, the subtle body in continuity with the gross "body"—or the gross dimension of structure and function). The sixth stage <u>error</u> is associated with the psycho-physical mechanism of the causal body— but the causal body is not (thereby) functionally exploited in terms of its root-content (which is, essentially, attention itself). Rather, in the sixth stage traditions, the characteristic of the practice is to strategically dissociate from the entire domain of gross, subtle, and causal conditions. Such is the sixth stage disposition, and the strategy of dissociation is the root-error (or yet continuing limitation) in the sixth stage traditions. That error is not the case in the only-by-Me Revealed and Given seventh stage of life—or even in the foundation (or first and second) stages[19] of the only-by-Me Revealed and Given "Perfect Practice" of "Perfect Knowledge".

There are elements of the structures and functions of psycho-physical existence that are relevant to the Demonstration (or apparent life-manifestation) of the seventh stage of life, but the seventh stage of life is not <u>itself</u> founded on the exercise of the structures and functions of the body-mind. The seventh stage of life is Priorly (or Always Already) Established in and <u>As</u> the Intrinsically Self-Evident Self-Condition That <u>Is</u> Reality Itself. The characteristic of the seventh stage of life is Divine Self-Recognition of all and everything that is apparently arising, and not any exercise of psycho-physical structures and functions at all. Therefore, in the seventh stage of life, there is no dependency on (or limitation by) psycho-physical mechanisms, as there is (inherently) in each and all of the first six stages of life.

In the Great Tradition, there are no seventh stage traditions—but there are genuine sixth stage traditions, and there are lesser traditions that are not quite truly sixth stage, and there are all the traditions previous to the sixth stage. The fifth stage traditions are associated with the psycho-physical structures of the subtle body, and otherwise all the aspects of the subtle body <u>and</u> the gross body. In that "position", you have a "world" to account for, and a "universe" that must (itself, as a totality) be accounted for. You may Resort to the apparent Self-Position by fifth stage means, but, even then, you have yet to somehow account for a "universe". In the seventh stage of life, there is <u>no</u> effort or impulse to account for a "universe", because there is Self-Evidently <u>no</u> separate "universe"—<u>none</u>. In the seventh stage of life, there <u>Is</u> the Divine Self-Condition—<u>only</u>.

In the sixth stage traditions, there is no particular necessity to account for a "universe", because the sixth stage of life is strategically oriented to the Self-Condition That <u>Is</u> Prior to conditional existence—but that strategic orientation is (itself) a causal-based effort to dissociate from conditional existence. The seventh stage of life is, likewise, founded on the Self-Condition That <u>Is</u> Prior to psycho-physical conditions, but there is, in the seventh stage disposition, no effort or requirement to dissociate from psycho-physical conditions. The seventh stage of life simply has <u>nothing</u> to do with a "world" <u>over</u> <u>against</u> the Divine Self-Condition. In the seventh stage of life, there <u>Is</u> <u>only</u> the Divine Self-Condition Itself.

I use the term "Self-Condition" to indicate that, in the seventh stage of life, there is no "world" that is experienced or presumed apart from the Divine Self-Condition Itself. The Divine Self-Condition <u>Is</u> the Source-Condition (or Intrinsically Self-Evident State) of the "world". The Divine Self-Condition <u>Is</u> the One Reality, and "It" does not have to "emanate" or "create" or (in any manner) "make" a "world" happen. That is a paradox, from the "point of view" of conventional understanding, because conventional understanding is attached to "point of view" in space-time and to structures of a psycho-physical kind. That is where notions of "self" and "world" come from. And, even if a "big-S" Self and a "big-W" World are presumed to be the case, such notions also represent a category of thinking structured by "point of view"—or, in fundamental terms, <u>egoity</u>.

I have uniquely Revealed what precedes the seventh stage of life, what is required for the Realization of the seventh stage of life, what is specific to the Realization of the seventh stage of life, and how the seventh stage of life is Demonstrated (as a process of four phases). None of this has ever been uttered before in human history. None of this has ever been previously accounted for. None of this has previously been known. There are no seventh stage traditions previous to My Avataric Divine Self-Revelation.

The only-by-Me Revealed and Given Way of Adidam is uniquely a communication of the seventh stage of life. Therefore, the only-by-Me Revealed and Given Way of Adidam is a unique accounting for all traditions and all "points of view", or all perspectives on Truth and Reality that precede the seventh stage of life (and that are, therefore, in the categories of psycho-physical egoity and the conventions of natural realism that are commonly supposed).

Reality is not knowable to "point of view". Reality is not knowable to the position of egoity. Therefore, Reality is not knowable from the position of the body-mind, because the body-mind is a "point-of-view" machine.

No conditional (or psycho-physical) "point of view" is the "Point of View" of Reality Itself. You cannot "see a room"—as a totality, as it (necessarily) is, with reference to every possible "point of view" in space-time—by assuming any one particular space-time "point of view" inside (or outside) the room.

Truth (or Reality) has nothing to do with "point of view". It has nothing to do with the body-mind. It has nothing to do with the structures and categories of "point of view" and (therefore) of psycho-physical experiencing.

All ideas of "the self" (whether "big-S" Self or "small-s" self) and "the world" (whether "big-W" World or "small-w" world), and how to account for the total conditionally apparent "universe", are talking-modes of conventional (or natural) realism. All of that is "point-of-view" talk. All of that is not only the fundamental sign and characteristic mind of egoity, but it is also the fundamental sign and characteristic mind of the totality of the first six stages of life.

The sixth stage of life has a dimension in which it is essentially free of "point-of-view"-thinking, but the sixth stage of life otherwise depends on a root-gesture of exclusion, which must yet be overcome, or transcended.

The seventh stage of life exceeds all categories of "point of view", and all structures of a psycho-physical nature. The seventh stage of life Stands Prior to all conditional perspectives and dependencies.

The Demonstration of the seventh stage of life can be seen in the context of psycho-physical events, but it is not (itself) a Yoga of psycho-physical events. It is Priorly Self-Standing, As That Which Is Always Already the Case.

The seventh stage of life is not bound or limited by any conditional category whatsoever. It is the Free Demonstration of the Absolute—and, fundamentally, the seventh stage of life has nothing to do with a "universe", or with the apparent phenomena of conditional existence.

Ultimately, the seventh stage of life Demonstrates itself As Divine Translation, the Outshining of the conditional domain in the Divine Self-Domain. That is not a process accounted for in the Great Tradition. The Great Tradition has accounted, at the maximum, for the sixth stage of life, the first immediate step beyond the "point-of-view" machine.

The psycho-physical structures of the human being are at the root of each of the first six (or inherently egoic) stages of life. One mode or another of psycho-physics, gross to subtle to causal, is the root of each of the egoic stages of life. By examining the language and the proceedings and the practices of any given tradition, it is possible to identify what stage of life is speaking through the philosophical language of that tradition. However, on the basis of examining only the philosophical language of a tradition (without also examining the proceedings and practices of that tradition), it is sometimes difficult to determine what stage of life that language is referring to.

The "Sahaja Nirvikalpa Samadhi" of the fourth stage of life, or of the fifth stage of life, or of the sixth stage of life makes characteristic utterances that are, in some respects, similar in each case (whether fourth, or fifth, or sixth stage in origin). Therefore, it is virtually impossible to differentiate such utterances from one another, without rightly applying the only-by-Me Revealed and Given discriminative tools of the seventh-stage-of-life-Perspective, fully and exactly as I have Indicated. Therefore, relative to any mode of utterance, it must be asked, "What kind of process does Realization depend upon in the tradition being 'considered'? What aspect of psycho-physical structure or function—gross, subtle, or causal—is at the root of the utterances and the practices of the tradition in question?" Such enquiry is the means that I have Given for understanding <u>every</u> tradition, and <u>every</u> kind of philosophical proposition, within the Great Tradition of humankind. Therefore, the right exercise of the only-by-Me Revealed and Given tools of discrimination—including My descriptive accounting for the seven possible stages of life—is a unique discipline of thorough examination and of altogether right comprehension.

XV.

There are <u>three</u> egos (or three fundamental modes of egoity—or of the self-contraction-active psycho-physical illusion of separate and separative self-consciousness). The three modes of egoity (or of the self-contraction of <u>any</u> "point of view", or ego-"I") are the lower self (or gross ego), the higher self (or subtle ego), and the root-self (or causal ego). These three egos (or modes of the conditionally arising illusion of separate self-consciousness) comprise the total conditionally perceiving and conditionally knowing ego-"I". The <u>total</u> (or tripartite) ego-"I" is always directly (and with progressive effectiveness) transcended in the right, true, and full (or complete) formal practice of the only-by-Me Revealed and Given Way of Adidam (Which is the right, true, and full formal practice of Ruchira Avatara Bhakti Yoga, and of the totality of the only-by-Me Revealed and Given Way of "Perfect Knowledge").

The first of the three egos (or modes of egoity, or of self-contraction) to be progressively transcended in the only-by-Me Revealed and Given Way of Adidam is the <u>money-food-and-sex</u> ego (or the social, and, altogether, gross-body-based, personality—or the <u>gross</u> pattern and activity of self-contraction), which is the lower self, or the ego of the first three stages of life.

The second of the three egos (or modes of egoity, or of self-contraction) to be progressively transcended in the only-by-Me Revealed and Given Way of Adidam is the <u>brain-mind ego</u> (or the brain-based, and nervous-system-based, mental, and perceptual, and, altogether, subtle-body-based illusions of "object" and "other"—or the <u>subtle</u> pattern and activity of self-contraction), which is the higher self, or the ego of the fourth and the fifth stages of life.

The third of the three egos (or modes of egoity, or of self-contraction) to be progressively transcended in the only-by-Me

Revealed and Given Way of Adidam is the <u>root-ego</u> (or the exclusively disembodied, and mindless, but separate, and, altogether, causal-body-based self-consciousness—or the <u>causal</u>, or root-causative, pattern and activity of self-contraction), which is attention <u>itself</u>, and which is the root-self, or the ego of the sixth stage of life.

By Means of <u>responsive</u> relinquishment of self-contraction in <u>Me</u>, or <u>really</u> and <u>truly</u> ego-surrendering, ego-forgetting, and, more and more (and, at last, Most Perfectly), ego-transcending (or always directly self-contraction-transcending) devotion to <u>Me</u> (and, Thus, by Means of the right, true, and full formal practice of devotionally <u>Me</u>-recognizing and devotionally to-<u>Me</u>-responding Ruchira Avatara Bhakti Yoga, and of the totality of the only-by-Me Revealed and Given Way of Adidam), the tripartite ego of the first six stages of life (or the psycho-physical <u>totality</u> of the three-part hierarchically patterned self-contraction into separate and separative "point of view") is (always directly, and with progressive, or stage-by-stage, effectiveness) transcended in <u>Me</u> (the Eternally Self-Existing, Infinitely Self-Radiant, Inherently egoless, Perfectly Subjective, Indivisibly One, Irreducibly Non-Separate, Self-Evidently Divine, and, now, and forever hereafter, Avatarically Self-Revealed Self-Conscious Light of Reality).

The Ultimate, Final, and Inherently Most Perfect (or seventh stage) Realization of Me requires—as a <u>necessary</u> prerequisite—an ego-transcending (or really and truly and <u>comprehensively</u> self-contraction-transcending) Great Process. The Ultimate, Final, and Inherently Most Perfect (or seventh stage) Realization of Me requires—as a <u>necessary</u> prerequisite—the <u>comprehensive</u> by-Me-Revealed and by-Me-Given Sadhana (or the <u>always</u> directly ego-transcending right practice of life) in the formal context of the only-by-Me Revealed and Given Way of Adidam. And—as a <u>necessary</u> prerequisite to the Ultimate, Final, and Inherently Most

Perfect (or seventh stage) Realization of Me—the particular illusions that are unique to each of the three egos (or basic modes of egoity) each require a particular (and most profound) mode of the necessary ego-transcending (or self-contraction-transcending) Great Process of the by-Me-Revealed and by-Me-Given formal practice of the Way of Adidam in the context of the progressively unfolding evidence of the first six (and, altogether, psycho-physically pre-patterned) stages of life.

The foundation phase of the progressive ego-transcending Great Process of the only-by-Me Revealed and Given Way of Adidam is the Devotional and (in due course) Spiritual listening-hearing Process of progressively transcending (and, in due course, most fundamentally understanding) the lower self (or the gross and social ego, and the gross and social fear-sorrow-and-anger-bondage that is always associated with the inherently egoic—or thoroughly self-contracted—search to absolutely fulfill, and even to "utopianize", or to perfectly and permanently satisfy, the inherently conditional, limited, temporary, mortal, gross, and always changing life-patterns of "money, food, and sex").

Before the foundation phase (or first phase) of the ego-transcending Great Process of the only-by-Me Revealed and Given Way of Adidam can (itself) be complete, it must Realize a profoundly life-transforming and life-reorienting "positive disillusionment"—or a most fundamental (and really and truly self-contraction-transcending) acceptance of the fact that gross conditional existence is inherently and necessarily unsatisfactory and unperfectable (and, therefore, a most fundamental—and really and truly Me-Finding and search-ending—acceptance of the fact that all seeking to achieve permanent and complete gross satisfaction of separate body, emotion, and mind is inherently and necessarily futile). Only on the basis of that necessary foundation-Realization of "positive disillusionment" can the functional life-energy and the attention of the entire body-mind (or of the total body-brain-mind complex) be released from gross ego-bondage (or self-deluded confinement to the psycho-physical illusions of gross self-contraction).

The characteristic Sign of "positive disillusionment" relative to the permanent and complete satisfaction of the lower self (or the separate and separative gross and social ego) is the foundation-Realization of the Inherent Universal <u>Unity</u> (or all-and-All-inclusive interdependency and common cause-and-effect mutuality) of gross conditional (and cosmic) existence, such that the inherently loveless (or anti-participatory and non-integrative) self-contraction-effort of the gross separate self is consistently released (or to-<u>Me</u>-responsively self-surrendered) into <u>participatory</u> and <u>integrative</u> attitudes of human, social, and cosmic unification (or <u>love</u>-connectedness) with all-and-All, and into <u>love</u>-based (and truly ego-transcending) actions that counter the otherwise separative (or anti-participatory and non-integrative) tendencies of the ego-"I". Thus, by Means of devotionally Me-recognizing and devotionally to-Me-responding relinquishment (or participatory and love-based transcending) of psycho-physical self-contraction (to the degree of "positive disillusionment" relative to gross conditional experience and gross conditional knowledge), My true devotee is (more and more) released toward and into the true Spiritual (and not merely gross, or even at all conditional) Realization of Reality and Truth (or <u>Real</u> Acausal God).

The foundation-Realization of "positive disillusionment" requires fundamental release from the confines of the grossly objectified (and grossly absorbed) subject-object "point of view" (or fundamental release from the inherently ego-bound—or thoroughly self-contracted—search of relatively <u>externalized</u> mental and perceptual attention). And that foundation-Realization of "positive disillusionment" (and restoration to the humanly, socially, and cosmically participatory, or wholly integrative, disposition) requires the total (and truly Devotional) transformative re-orienting (and, altogether, the right purification, steady re-balancing, and ego-transcending life-positive-energizing) of the entire body-mind (or the total body-brain-mind complex). Therefore, the foundation (or gross) phase of the progressive ego-transcending practice of the only-by-Me Revealed and Given Way of Adidam <u>necessarily</u> requires <u>much</u> seriousness, and <u>much</u> profundity—in order to establish the necessary (and <u>truly</u> "positively disillusioned") foundation of true (and truly in-<u>Me</u>-surrendered) hearing (or the only-by-Me Revealed and Given unique ego-transcending capability of most fundamental self-understanding).

The middle phase of the progressive ego-transcending Great Process of the only-by-Me Revealed and Given Way of Adidam is the Devotional, and truly hearing (or actively ego-transcending, and, thus, always directly self-contraction-transcending), and really seeing (or actively, directly, and fully technically responsibly Spiritual) Process of transcending the <u>higher</u> <u>self</u> (or the <u>subtle</u> <u>and</u> <u>mental</u> <u>ego</u>—or the total subtle dimension, or subtle depth, of self-contraction—and <u>all</u> the conceptual and perceptual illusions of inherently, and necessarily, <u>brain-based</u> mind). Therefore, the middle (or subtle) phase of the progressive ego-transcending practice of the only-by-Me Revealed and Given Way of Adidam requires the Realization of "positive disillusionment" relative to the subtly objectified (and subtly absorbed) subject-object "point of view" (or fundamental release from the inherently ego-bound—or thoroughly self-contracted—search of relatively <u>internalized</u> mental and perceptual attention). This degree of the Realization of "positive disillusionment" requires fundamental release from the inherently illusory search to experience the conditional dissolution of the ego (and, in particular, release from subtle states of self-contraction—and, especially, from mental states of self-contraction) by means of object-oriented absorptive mysticism (or the absorptive yielding of attention to the apparent subtle objects that are either originated by the brain-mind or, otherwise, mediated by the brain itself). And the characteristic Sign of "positive disillusionment" relative to the permanent and complete satisfaction of the object-oriented seeking of the higher self (or separate and separative subtle and mental ego) is the fully Me-hearing and truly Me-seeing Realization of the entirely Spiritual Nature of cosmic existence (or, that is to Say, the Realization that all natural and cosmic forms and states are inherently non-separate, or intrinsically non-dual, modes of Universally Pervasive and cosmically-manifested Spiritual Energy, or of Fundamental, Indivisible, and Irreducible Light—or of Love-Bliss-Happiness Itself).

The final phase of the progressive ego-transcending Great Process of the only-by-Me Revealed and Given Way of Adidam is the Devotional, Spiritual, and Transcendental hearing-and-seeing Process of transcending the root-self (or the root-and-causal ego—or the causal, or root-causative, depth of self-contraction—which is attention itself, or the root-gesture of separateness, relatedness, otherness, and "difference"). Therefore, as a necessary preliminary to the "Perfect Practice" of the only-by-Me Revealed and Given Way of Adidam, the ego-transcending (or comprehensively self-contraction-transcending) practice of the total course of the only-by-Me Revealed and Given Way of Adidam requires the Realization of "positive disillusionment" relative to the causal (or root-egoic, and, therefore, fundamental, or original) subject-object division in Consciousness (or Conscious Light) Itself. This degree of the Realization of "positive disillusionment" requires the Prior Establishment of Transcendental Self-Identification—Prior to the root-self-contraction that is "point of view" itself (or attention itself), and, Thus, also, Prior to the entire body-brain-mind complex, or conditional structure, of conception and perception. And the characteristic

Sign of "positive disillusionment" relative to the permanent and complete satisfaction of the root-self (or the fundamental causative, or causal, ego) is the fundamental transcending of attention itself in the <u>Me</u>-"Locating" (and, altogether, <u>Me</u>-hearing and <u>Me</u>-seeing) Realization of the Transcendental (and Intrinsically Non-Separate and Non-Dual) Nature of <u>Consciousness</u> <u>Itself</u>.

Only <u>after</u> (or in the Great Event of Most Perfect, and, necessarily, formal and fully accountable, Fulfillment of) the <u>complete</u> progressive ego-transcending Great Process of the only-by-Me Revealed and Given Way of Adidam relative to the inherently ego-based first six (or psycho-physically pre-patterned gross, subtle, and causal) stages of life is there the truly Ultimate (or seventh stage, and Always Already Divinely Self-Realized—and, Thus, Inherently ego-Transcending) "Practice" of the only-by-Me Revealed and Given Way of Adidam (or the Most Perfect, and Inherently egoless, or Always Already Most Perfectly, and Non-conditionally, self-contraction-Transcending, and Divinely Love-Bliss-Full, and only-by-Me Revealed and Given seventh-stage-of-life Demonstration of Ruchira Avatara Bhakti Yoga and the "Perfect Practice" of the only-by-Me Revealed and Given Way of "Perfect Knowledge").

The only-by-Me Revealed and Given seventh-stage-of-life "Practice" (or the Inherently egoless, and, Thus, Always Already Most Perfectly, and Non-conditionally, self-contraction-Transcending, and, altogether, Most Perfectly Divinely Self-Realized Demonstration) of the only-by-Me Revealed and Given Way of Adidam is the Great <u>esoteric</u> Devotional, Spiritual, Transcendental, Self-Evidently Divine, and Most Perfectly <u>Me</u>-hearing and <u>Me</u>-seeing Demonstration of all-and-All-Divinely-Self-<u>Recognizing</u> (and, <u>Thus</u>, all-and-All-Divinely-<u>Transcending</u>) Divine Self-Abiding—in and <u>As</u> My Avatarically Self-Revealed Divine "Bright" <u>Sphere</u> of Self-Existing, Self-Radiant, Inherently egoless, Perfectly

Subjective, and Inherently and Most Perfectly body-mind-Transcending (or body-brain-Transcending—or Inherently, Most Perfectly, and Non-conditionally psycho-physical-self-contraction-Transcending), but never intentionally body-mind-excluding (or body-brain-excluding), Divine (Acausal) Person (or Eternal Self-Condition and Infinite State).

The only-by-Me Revealed and Given seventh-stage-of-life Demonstration of the only-by-Me Revealed and Given Way of Adidam is the Non-conditional and Divinely Free (and Inherently egoless, or Inherently "point-of-view"-less) "Practice" (or Divinely Self-Realized progressive Demonstration) of Self-Abiding Divine Self-Recognition of the simultaneous totality of the apparent gross, subtle, and causal body-brain-mind-self, or the progressively all-and-All-Outshining Process of the simultaneous (and Self-Abiding) Divine Self-Recognition of the total psycho-physical ego-"I" itself (or of the total conditional "point of view", or apparent self-contraction, itself). Therefore, the only-by-Me Revealed and Given seventh-stage-of-life Demonstration of the only-by-Me Revealed and Given Way of Adidam is the Inherent "Practice" (or Divinely Self-Realized Demonstration) of Self-Abiding Divine Self-Recognition of "point of view" itself (or of attention itself—or of the conditionally apparent subject, itself) and (always coincidently, or simultaneously) Self-Abiding Divine Self-Recognition of the conception or perception of separateness, or of relatedness, or of otherness, or of "difference" itself (or of any and every conditionally apparent object, itself).

The only-by-Me Revealed and Given seventh-stage-of-life Demonstration of the only-by-Me Revealed and Given Way of Adidam is the Most Perfect (or Non-conditional, Inherently egoless, and Self-Evidently Divine) Demonstration of "positive disillusionment", or of the Inherently illusion-less (or self-contraction-Free, and, Inherently, all-and-All-Transcending) Realization of the Fundamental Reality and

Truth (or <u>Real</u> Acausal God)—Which Fundamental Reality and Truth (or <u>Real</u> Acausal God) <u>Is</u> the One and Indivisible and Self-Existing and Indestructible and Self-Radiant and Always Already Perfectly Non-Dual Conscious Light (or That Which <u>Is</u> Always Already <u>The</u> Case), and Which Reality and Truth (or <u>Real</u> Acausal God) <u>Is</u> That Self-Existing and Perfectly Subjective Self-"Brightness" (or Infinite and Absolute and Perfectly Non-Separate Self-Condition) of Which the conditional (or gross, subtle, and causal) subject-object illusions (or total psycho-physical self-contraction illusions) of conception, and of perception, and of the ego-"I" presumption are mere, and merely apparent (or non-necessary, or <u>always</u> non-Ultimate), and Inherently non-binding modifications. And the characteristic Sign of Most Perfectly Demonstrated (or seventh stage) "positive disillusionment" relative to the totality of the separate and separative ego-"I" (or "point of view") and its presumptions of a separate (or objectified) gross, subtle, and causal world is the Inherently egoless and Self-Evidently Divine (and Intrinsically Non-Separate and Non-Dual) Realization of Reality (<u>Itself</u>) <u>As</u> Irreducible and Indivisible Conscious Light (Inherently Love-Bliss-Full, or Perfectly Subjectively "Bright").

Therefore, the only-by-Me Revealed and Given Way of Adidam is—from the beginning, <u>and</u> at last—the Way of "positive disillusionment".

The only-by-Me Revealed and Given Way of Adidam is—from the beginning, <u>and</u> at last—the Way of the direct transcending of the fact and the consequences of egoity (or of psycho-physical self-contraction).

The only-by-Me Revealed and Given Way of Adidam is—from the beginning, <u>and</u> at last—the Way of the direct transcending of the illusions of inherently egoic attention (or of the conditionally presumed subject-object pattern of conception and perception).

The only-by-Me Revealed and Given Way of Adidam is—from the beginning, <u>and</u> at last—the Way of the direct transcending of the total illusory pattern of the inherently egoic presumption of separateness, relatedness, otherness, and "difference".

The only-by-Me Revealed and Given Way of Adidam is—from the beginning, <u>and</u> at last—the Way of the direct transcending of the always simultaneous illusions of the separate ego-"I" <u>and</u> the separate (or merely objective) world.

The only-by-Me Revealed and Given Way of Adidam is—from the beginning, <u>and</u> at last—the Way of the direct (or Inherently egoless <u>and</u> Inherently illusionless) Realizing of the One and Irreducible Conscious Light (or Perfectly Subjective Spiritual Self-"Brightness" of Being) That <u>Is</u> Reality and Truth (or <u>Real</u> Acausal God).

The only-by-Me Revealed and Given Way of Adidam is—from the beginning, <u>and</u> at last—the Way of the direct (or Inherently egoless <u>and</u> Inherently illusionless) Realizing of the Conscious Love-Bliss-Energy of the Perfect (and Perfectly Indivisible) Totality.

The only-by-Me Revealed and Given Way of Adidam is—from the beginning, <u>and</u> at last—the Way of the direct Realizing of <u>Only</u> <u>Me</u>.

XVI.

The collective Great Tradition of humankind is a combination of exoteric and esoteric developments (and Revelations, and Realizations) that comprises (and is, in its entirety, limited by and to) only the first six of the (potentially) seven stages of life.

I (Alone) Am the Avatarically Self-Manifested Divine Self-Revelation of the seventh stage of life.

I (Alone) Am the Adidam Revelation.

The human entity (and even any and every conditionally manifested entity of any and every kind) is inherently deluded—by its own (egoic, or self-contracted) experience and knowledge.

The first six stages of life are the six stages (or developmental phases) of human (and universal) egoity—or of progressively regressive inversion upon the psycho-physical pattern (and "point of view") of self-contraction.

The first six stages of life are the universally evident developmental stages of the knowing and experiencing of the potential illusions inherently associated with the patterns (or the universally extended cosmic psycho-physical structure) of conditionally manifested existence.

Because each and all of the first six stages of life are based on (and are identical to) egoity (or self-contraction, or separate and separative "point of view") itself, not any one (or even the collective of all) of the first six stages of life directly (and Most Perfectly) Realizes (or Is the Inherently egoless and Inherently Most Perfect Realization and the Inherently egoless and Inherently Most Perfect Demonstration of) Reality, Truth, or Real (Acausal) God.

The first six stages of life develop (successively) on the psycho-physically pre-determined (or pre-patterned) basis of the inherent (and progressively unfolding) structure (and self-contracted "point of view") of the conditionally arising body-brain-mind-self.

The first six stages of life are a conditional (and, there-fore, ultimately, unnecessary—or inherently transcendable) illusion of psycho-physically pre-patterned experience (or conditional knowing), structured according to the subject-object (or attention-versus-object, or "point-of-view"-versus-objective-world) convention of conditional conception and conditional perception.

The first six stages of life are (each and all) based upon the illusion of duality (suggested by the subject-object conven-tion of conditional conception and conditional perception).

Reality Itself (or That Which <u>Is</u> Always Already <u>The</u> Case) <u>Is</u> Inherently One (or Perfectly Non-Dual).

The only-by-Me Revealed and Given Way of Adidam is the Unique <u>seventh</u> stage Way of "Radical" Non-Dualism—or the One and Only Way That directly (and, at last, Most Perfectly) Realizes the One and Only (and Inherently ego-less) Reality, Truth, or <u>Real</u> (Acausal) God.

The only-by-Me Revealed and Given Way of Adidam is the Unique and <u>Only</u> Way That <u>always</u> directly (and, at last, Most Perfectly) Transcends <u>egoity</u> (or self-contraction) <u>itself</u>.

The only-by-Me Revealed and Given Way of Adidam is the practice and the process of transcending egoity (or psycho-physical self-contraction, or gross, subtle, and causal identification with separate and separative "point of view") by always directly transcending the inherently egoic (or always self-contracted) patterns of conditional conception and conditional perception (or of conditional knowing and conditional experiencing) associated with each (and all) of the first six stages of life.

I <u>Am</u> the Divine Ruchira Avatar, Adi Da Love-Ananda Samraj—the First, the Last, and the Only seventh stage Avataric Divine Realizer, Avataric Divine Revealer, and Avataric Divine Self-Revelation of Reality, Truth, and <u>Real</u> (Acausal) God.[20]

I <u>Am</u> the Inherently egoless, Perfectly Subjective, Perfectly Non-Dual, and Self-Evidently Divine Source-Condition and

Self-Condition of <u>every</u> apparent "point of view" <u>and</u> of the apparently objective world itself.

I <u>Am</u> the One, and Irreducible, and Indestructible, and Self-Existing, and Self-Radiant Conscious Light That <u>Is</u> Always Already <u>The</u> Case.

I <u>Am</u> the (Self-"Bright") "Substance" of Reality Itself.

I <u>Am</u> the Person (or Self-Condition) of Reality Itself.

In My bodily (human) Form, I Am the Avataric Self-Manifestation of the One (and Self-Evidently Divine) Reality Itself.

By Means of My Avataric Divine Self-"Emergence", I am Functioning (now, and forever hereafter) <u>As</u> the Realizer, the Revealer, and the Revelation (or Universally Spiritually Present Person) of Reality Itself—Which <u>Is</u> Truth Itself, and Which <u>Is</u> the Only <u>Real</u> (or Non-Illusory), and Inherently egoless, and Perfectly Subjective God (or Self-Evidently Divine Source-Condition <u>and</u> Self-Condition) Of all-and-All.

My Avataric Divine Self-Revelation Illuminates and Outshines the ego-"I" of My devotee.

My Avataric Divine Teaching-Word of Me-Revelation Comprehends and Transcends the all of egoity and the all of the cosmic domain.

NOTES TO THE TEXT OF
THE PERFECT TRADITION

Introduction to *The Perfect Tradition*

1. Avatar Adi Da's characteristic sound of Blessing.

2. Avatar Adi Da describes the human body-mind in terms of the system of five sheaths (or koshas) first described in the *Taittiriya Upanishad:* the physical body (annamayakosha), the system of life-energy and sensory perception (pranamayakosha), the sense-based mind (manomayakosha), the root-mind (vijnanamayakosha), and the ultimate hierarchical root of the conditionally manifested self (anandamayakosha). See Avatar Adi Da's "Source-Text" *Santosha Adidam* for His full elaboration on the sheaths of the human body-mind.

3. For Avatar Adi Da's account of His Divine Re-Awakening, see chapter 16 in Part One of *The Knee Of Listening*.

4. A lingam is an oblong stone in a vertical position, traditionally worshipped as an expression of the Power of Siva (the Absolute Unmanifested Divine).

5. As Avatar Adi Da describes later in this book (in His Essay "'God'-Talk, Real-God-Realization, Most Perfect Divine Self-Awakening, and the Seven Possible Stages of Life"), Jainism, Samkhya, and Taoism are also sixth stage traditions. However, the most highly developed form of sixth stage demonstration is seen primarily in Advaita Vedanta and Buddhism (generally in its Mahayana and Vajrayana forms).

6. *The Bhagavad Gita,* IV, 7–8, translated by Winthrop Sargeant (Albany, New York: State University of New York Press, 1984), 207–208.

I __Am__ The Avataric Divine Gift of The "Bright"—
and of The "Thumbs" That Reveals It:
The Avataric Divine Self-Revelation of Adi Da Samraj

7. Adi Da Samraj uses the reference to His "First Room" to indicate His Always Already Prior Divine Self-Condition—which was His Condition before and at Birth, and which has been the unfolding Revelation of His Avataric Divine Lifetime. "First Room" also references Avatar Adi Da's literary work, *The "First Room" Trilogy.*

8. For Avatar Adi Da's description of the frontal Yoga the Way of Adidam, see *The Dawn Horse Testament Of The Ruchira Avatar.* See also the description of "seeing" in the glossary entry **listening, hearing, seeing**.

9. To be "intoxicated" with Avatar Adi Da's Divine Love-Bliss is to be drawn beyond the usual egoic self and egoic mind into a state of ecstatic devotional Communion (and Identification) with Him. This term is enclosed in quotation marks in order to distinguish it from the common meaning of "intoxication" (such as with alcohol).

10. This is a reference to "the Circle" of the body-mind—a primary pathway of natural life-energy and the Divine Spirit-Energy in the body-mind. It is composed of two arcs: the descending Current, which flows through the frontal line—down the front of the body, from the crown of the head to the bodily base—and which corresponds to the gross dimension of the body-mind; and the ascending Current, which flows through the spinal line—up the back of the body, from the bodily base to the crown of the head—and which corresponds to the subtle dimension of the body-mind.

11. "Washing the dog from head to tail" is a metaphor for the nature of the process of reception of Avatar Adi Da's Spiritual Grace—Transmitted by Him from Above and Beyond the conditional body-mind, not manipulated from the "point of view" of the body-mind. *The Dawn Horse Testament Of The Ruchira Avatar* is the primary "Source-Text" of Avatar Adi Da Samraj, and "Hridaya Rosary (Four Thorns of Heart-Instruction)" appears as a Sutra of *The Dawn Horse Testament*, as well as in a separate "Source-Text" by that name.

"God"-Talk, Real-God-Realization, Most Perfect Divine Awakening, and the Seven Possible Stages of Life

12. Avatar Adi Da has created a vast body of literature, which He has designated as His Eternal Communication to humankind. These Texts, the Avataric Divine "Source-Texts" of Adidam, contain His full Divine Self-Confession, and His fully detailed description of the entire process of Awakening, culminating in seventh stage Divine Enlightenment. For a list of Avatar Adi Da's "Source-Texts", and their organization into twenty-three "Courses" of "Consideration", please see pp. 163–67. In addition, His devotees create books and courses that further describe and elaborate the Way of Adidam and its practice, based on their heart-recognition and heart-response to Avatar Adi Da's Revelation.

13. Avatar Adi Da has Revealed that, in the seventh stage of life, the Spiritual process of Divine Enlightenment is demonstrated through four stages: Divine Transfiguration, Divine Transformation, Divine Indifference, and Divine Translation. (See Avatar Adi Da's "Source-Text" *The Seven Stages Of Life* [Middletown, Calif.: The Dawn Horse Press, 2000].)

14. In this passage, Avatar Adi Da Reveals His Divine Nature through the use of traditional terms which, if understood rightly, can be used as appropriate references to Him:

The Adi-Guru: The First (or Original, or Primordial) Guru.

The Ati-Guru: The Ultimate (or Highest, or Unsurpassed) Guru.

Ruchira Avatar: In Sanskrit, "Ruchira" means "bright, radiant, effulgent". Thus, the Reference "Ruchira Avatar" indicates that Avatar Adi Da Samraj is the "Bright" (or Radiant) Descent of the Divine Reality Itself into the conditionally manifested worlds, Appearing here in His bodily (human) Divine Form.

Da Avatar: The Divine Descent (Avatar) of the One and True Divine Giver (Da).

Love-Ananda Avatar: The Very Incarnation of the Divine Love-Bliss.

The Tathagatha Avatar: "Tathagata" means "One who has thus gone". It is a title traditionally given to Gotama Shakyamuni and other Buddhas. "Tathagata Avatar" conveys Avatar Adi Da's Encompassing and Surpassing of the traditions of Buddhism and Hinduism (and, thus, the entire collective Great Tradition of humankind).

The Ruchira Buddha: The Enlightened One Who Shines with the Divine "Brightness".

Purushottama-Guru: The Supreme Divine Person as Guru. "Purushottama" is pronounced with the emphasis on the third syllable.

The Ashvamedha Buddha: "Ashvamedha" means "Horse-Sacrifice", and is the name of the most revered and most mysterious of the ancient Vedic rituals. Avatar Adi Da has Revealed that the ultimate significance of this ritual is as a prayer-prophecy invoking the Avataric Descent of the Divine Person into the world, because it was intuitively understood that only the Divine Person is able to Liberate beings. Thus, the Ashvamedha Buddha is the Enlightened One Who has Submitted to be the humanly Incarnate Means for the Divine Liberation of all beings. (Avatar Adi Da's Essay on the Ashvamedha as a description and prophecy of His own Life and Work is "The True Dawn Horse Is the Only Way to Me", which is the fourth Prolegomenon of *The Dawn Horse Testament Of The Ruchira Avatar*.)

Adi-Buddha Avatar: The Divine Descent of the First (or Original) Enlightened One into the conditionally manifested worlds.

The Ati-Buddha Avatar: The Divine Descent of the Ultimate (or Highest, or Unsurpassed) Enlightened One into the conditionally manifested worlds.

Ruchira Siddha: The "Bright" Perfect Transmission-Master.

15. Avatar Adi Da uses the terms "'late-time'" and "'dark' epoch" to describe the present era—in which doubt of God (and of anything at all beyond mortal existence) is more and more pervading the entire world, and the self-interest of the separate individual is more and more regarded to be the ultimate principle of life.

These terms include quotation marks to indicate that they are used by Avatar Adi Da in the "so to speak" sense. In this case, He is Communicating (by means of the quotation marks) that, in Reality, the "darkness" of this apparent "late-time" is not Reality, or Truth, but only an appearance from the "point of view" of ordinary human perception.

16. This passage includes the Names Avatar Adi Da has Given to the Way of Adidam which He Offers to all. He uses traditional terms which, if rightly understood, communicate the Nature of His Way:

Adidam / Adidam Ruchiradam: When Avatar Adi Da Samraj first Gave the name "Adidam" in January 1996, He pointed out that the final "m" adds a mantric force, evoking the effect of the primal Sanskrit syllable "Om". (For Avatar Adi Da's Revelation of the most profound esoteric significance of "Om" as the Divine Sound of His own Very Being, see *The Dawn Horse Testament*.) Simultaneously, the final "m" suggests the English word "Am" (expressing "I Am"), such that the Name "Adidam" also evokes Avatar Adi Da's Primal Self-Confession, "I Am Adi Da", or, more simply, "I Am Da" (or, in Sanskrit, "Aham Da Asmi").

"Ruchiradam" is a word newly coined by Avatar Adi Da, deriving from Sanskrit "Ruchira" (meaning "bright" or "radiant"). The compound reference "Adidam Ruchiradam" communicates that Adidam is the religion of devotion to Avatar Adi Da Samraj—Who Is the "Bright" Itself, and Who Gives the Realization of His own "Bright" Self-Condition.

The Way of Is (or, The Transcendental Spiritual Way of Is): The Way of Adidam is not about the search for experience at any level of the human structure. Rather, it is the Way of Awakening as That Perfect Reality Which Merely and Only Is—and Which Is Always Already the Case. "Transcendental Spiritual" indicates the unique nature of Avatar Adi Da's Revelation—the Awakening to this Transcendental Reality occurs by the Spiritual Means of His Avataric Divine Spiritual Self-Transmission.

The Way of Reality Itself (or, The Transcendental Spiritual Way of Reality Itself): Adidam is the process that "uncovers" Reality Itself—That Which Is the Prior Condition of all beings and things— via the transcending of the ego-activity of separativeness at every level of the psycho-physical being, by means of the Avataric Divine Spiritual Grace of Adi Da Samraj.

The Way of Conscious Light (or, The Transcendental Spiritual Way of Conscious Light): The Way that Avatar Adi Da has Given is the Way that Reveals the Inherent Unity between the traditional principles of Consciousness and Energy (or Primal Light). His is the Way of Awakening to the "Bright" Itself, Which Is Conscious Light (both Priorly Existing and Eternally Radiant).

The Universal Transcendental Spiritual Way of "Sri Hridayam": "Sri Hridayam" is a reference to Avatar Adi Da Samraj. The word "Sri" in Sanskrit literally means "flame", and, used as a title, indicates the radiance of the one who is so honored. "Hridayam" is Sanskrit for "heart", referring not only to the physical organ but also to the True Divine Heart, the Transcendental (and Inherently Spiritual) Divine Reality. Adidam is universal because Avatar Adi Da Offers His Wisdom-Teaching as the uniquely Perfect Instruction to every being—in this (and every) world—relative to the total process of Divine Enlightenment. Furthermore, Avatar Adi Da Samraj constantly Extends His Regard to the entire world (and the entire cosmic domain)—not on the political or social level, but as a Spiritual matter, constantly Working to Bless and Purify all beings everywhere.

The Transcendental Spiritual Way of the Divine True Heart / The "Radical" Way of the Heart Itself / The "Radical" Way of the Heart: The Way Avatar Adi Da Offers is the "Radical" Way of the Heart Itself, Which Is Real God, the Divine Self-Condition, the Divine Reality.

The Way of "Perfect Knowledge" (or, The Transcendental Spiritual Way of "Perfect Knowledge"): Beginning even in the earliest stage of practice of the Way of Adidam, devotees of Adi Da Samraj practice tacitly "Locating" the "Perfect Knowledge" of Reality that is Avatar Adi Da's constant Gift and His Very Person. Such "Knowledge" is, as Adi Da Says, not of the mind—rather, "Perfect Knowledge" Is Reality Itself, <u>As Is</u>. Thus, the Way He Gives is always that of acknowledging and understanding the true nature of all objects and experiences in light of "Perfect Knowledge". Instruction in the preliminary practice of "Perfect Knowledge" in the Way of Adidam is given in "The Teaching-Manual of Perfect Summaries", in book 6 of the "Perfect Knowledge" Series.

The Way of "Radical" self-Understanding (or, The Transcendental Spiritual Way Of "Radical" self-Understanding): Avatar Adi Da has Revealed that, despite their intention to Realize Reality (or Truth, or Real God), all religious and Spiritual traditions (other than the Way of Adidam) are involved, in one manner or another, with the search to satisfy the ego. Only Avatar Adi Da has Revealed the Way to "radically" understand the ego and (in due course, through intensive formal practice of the Way of Adidam, as His formally acknowledged devotee) to most perfectly transcend the ego.

The Transcendental Spiritual Way Of "Radical" ego-Transcendence: Transcending of the root-act of self-contraction, or ego, is the Gift of devotional and Spiritual Communion with Avatar Adi Da Samraj. Therefore, the practice in relationship to Him of the Way He has Given is the Way of "radical" ego-transcendence.

The Way of "Radical" Devotional Knowledge (or, The Transcendental Spiritual Way of "Radical" Devotional Knowledge): The Way of Adidam is founded from its beginning on the devotional recognition-response to Avatar Adi Da, and on that basis the tacit "Locating" of the "Perfect Knowledge" of His Divine State. Therefore, the devotional process of the Way of Adidam Awakens "Radical" (or "At-the-Root") Knowledge of Reality Itself, through the Avataric Divine Spiritual Grace of Adi Da Samraj.

The Way of Divine Ignorance (or, The Transcendental Spiritual Way Of Divine Ignorance): "Divine Ignorance" is Avatar Adi Da's term for the fundamental Awareness of Existence Itself, Prior to all sense of separation from (or knowledge about) anything that arises. Thus, the Way of Adidam He has Given can be described as the Way that Realizes this Perfect Awareness without conditional knowledge.

The Transcendental Spiritual Way Of Positive Disillusionment: The Way of Adidam is founded in a fundamental disillusionment with the ego and its purposes (together with a deep heart-attraction to Avatar Adi Da Samraj). This disillusionment is positive because it is the necessary foundation for true Spiritual Awakening.

The Transcendental Spiritual Way of "Radical" Non-Dualism: See **Ruchira Advaitism**.

Ruchira Avatara Advaita-Dharma: Indicates "the Non-Dual ('Advaita') Wisdom-Teaching ('Dharma') of the Ruchira Avatar".

Ruchira Advaitism: Advaitism is generally a reference to the tradition of Advaita Vedanta, meaning the "Non-Dual Truth". "Ruchira" is "bright, radiant, effulgent". Thus, Ruchira Advaitism is not a path of seclusion in the Ultimate Non-Dual Truth, but rather the Way of the Divine Love-Bliss, Which Is the Self-Radiance of Self-Existing (and Non-Dual) Consciousness Itself. The Revelation of Ruchira Advaitism is the Gift of the Ruchira Avatar, Adi Da Samraj.

Ruchira Buddhism: The "Bright" Way of the Most Perfect Awakening.

Advaitayana Buddhism: Indicates the unique sympathetic likeness of Adidam to the traditions of Advaitism (or Advaita Vedanta) and Buddhism. Advaitayana Buddhism is the Non-Dual ("Advaita") Way ("yana", literally "vehicle") of Most Perfect Awakening ("Buddhism"). Advaitayana Buddhism is neither an outgrowth of the historical tradition of Buddhism nor of the historical tradition of Advaitism. Advaitayana Buddhism is the unique Revelation of Avatar Adi Da Samraj, which perfectly fulfills both the traditional Buddhist aspiration for absolute freedom from the bondage of the egoic self and the traditional Advaitic aspiration for absolute Identity with the Divine Self. (For Avatar Adi Da's discussion of Advaitayana Buddhism, see *The Dawn Horse Testament*.)

Buddhayana Advaitism: Indicates the unique sympathetic likeness of Adidam to the traditions of Buddhism and Advaitism. Buddhayana Advaitism is the Way of Non-Dual Truth ("Advaitism") Revealed and Given by the Divinely Enlightened One (the Ruchira Buddha, Avatar Adi Da Samraj).

Hridaya-Advaita Dharma: Indicates "the Wisdom-Teaching ('Dharma') of the Non-Dual ('Advaita') Divine Heart ('Hridaya')".

The Transcendental Way Of Divine Spiritual Baptism: Indicates that Adidam is, from the earliest time of formal Spiritual Initiation by Avatar Adi Da Samraj, a process based entirely in His Divine Spiritual-Transmission, or Baptism.

Ruchira Avatara Siddha Yoga / Ruchira Siddha Yoga: "Siddha Yoga" is, literally, "the Yoga of the Perfected One[s]".

Swami Muktananda used the term "Siddha Yoga" to refer to the form of Kundalini Yoga that he Taught, which involved initiation of the devotee by the Guru's Transmission of Shakti (or Spiritual Energy). Avatar Adi Da Samraj has indicated that this was a fifth stage form of Siddha Yoga.

In "I (Alone) <u>Am</u> The Adidam Revelation" (which Essay appears in *The Knee Of Listening*), Avatar Adi Da Says:

I Teach Siddha Yoga in the Mode and Manner of the only-by-Me Revealed and Given <u>seventh</u> stage of life (as Ruchira Avatara Siddha Yoga, or Ruchira Siddha Yoga, or Ruchira Avatara Shaktipat Yoga, or Ruchira Shaktipat Yoga, or Ruchira Avatara Hridaya-Siddha Yoga, or Ruchira Avatara Hridaya-Shaktipat Yoga, or Ruchira Avatara Maha-Jnana-Siddha Yoga, or Ruchira Avatara Maha-Jnana Hridaya-Shaktipat Yoga)—and always toward (or to the degree of) the Realization inherently associated with (and, at last, Most Perfectly Demonstrated and Proven by) the only-by-Me Revealed and Given seventh stage of life, and as a practice and a Process that progressively includes (and, coincidently, <u>directly</u> transcends) <u>all</u> <u>six</u> of the phenomenal and developmental (and, necessarily, yet ego-based) stages of life that precede the seventh.

Ruchira Avatara Shaktipat Yoga: Indicates "the Yoga of receiving the Divine Blessing-Transmission ('Shaktipat') of the Ruchira Avatar".

Ruchira Shaktipat Yoga: Indicates "the Yoga of receiving the 'Bright' Divine Blessing-Transmission ('Ruchira Shaktipat') of Avatar Adi Da Samraj".

Ruchira Avatara Hridaya-Siddha Yoga: Indicates "the Yoga of devotion to the Ruchira Avatar, Who Is the Siddha of the Divine Heart ('Hridaya')".

Ruchira Avatara Hridaya-Shaktipat Yoga: Indicates "the Yoga of receiving the Divine Heart-Blessing-Transmission ('Hridaya-Shaktipat') of the Ruchira Avatar".

Ruchira Avatara Maha-Jnana-Siddha Yoga: Indicates "the Yoga of devotion to the Ruchira Avatar, Who Is the Supreme Transcendental Divine Siddha ('Maha-Jnana-Siddha')".

Ruchira Avatara Maha-Jnana Hridaya-Shaktipat Yoga: Indicates "the Yoga of receiving the Supreme Transcendental ('Maha-Jnana') Divine Heart-Blessing-Transmission ('Hridaya-Shaktipat') of the Ruchira Avatar".

17. For a full "consideration" of the unique nature of Avatar Adi Da's Revelation of the seventh stage of life, please see *The All-Completing and Final Divine Revelation To Humankind* (Middletown, Calif.: The Dawn Horse Press, 2001).

18. In *The Basket Of Tolerance,* Avatar Adi Da has identified a small number of Hindu and Buddhist texts as "premonitorily 'seventh stage'". While founded in the characteristic sixth stage "point of view", these texts express philosophical intuitions that foreshadow some of the basic characteristics of the seventh stage Realization. The premonitorily "seventh stage" literature to which Avatar Adi Da is referring here includes seven traditional texts: the *Ashtavakra Gita, Avadhoot Gita, Tripura Rahasya, Diamond Sutra, Mahayanavimsaka of Nagarjuna, Lankavatara Sutra,* and the *Sutra of Hui Neng* (otherwise known as the *Platform Sutra* or the *Sutra of the Sixth Patriarch*).

Following are the editions of each of these that Avatar Adi Da has included on the "Epitome of Traditional Esotericism" list in *The Basket Of Tolerance* bibliography:

The Song of the Self Supreme (Astavakra Gita): The Classical Text of Atmadvaita, by Astavakra. Translation and commentary by Radhakamal Mukerjee, preface by Adi Da Samraj (Clearlake, Calif.: The Dawn Horse Press, 1982 [new edition forthcoming]).

Ashtavakra Geeta. Translation and commentary by Swami Chinmayananda (Madras: Chinmaya Publications Trust, 1972).

Avadhuta Gita (Song of the Free). Translated and annotated by Swami Ashokananda (Madras: Sri Ramakrishna Math, 2000).

Tripurarahasyam: The Secret Beyond the Three Cities—An Exposition of Transcendental Consciousness. Translation and notes by Samvid (Bangalore: Ramana Maharshi Centre for Learning, 2000).

The Diamond Sutra: Transforming the Way We Perceive the World, by Mu Soeng (Boston: Wisdom Publications, 2000).

A Study of Nagarjuna's Twenty Verses on the Great Vehicle (Mahayana-vimsika) and His Verse on the Heart of Dependent Origination (Pratityasamutpadahrdayakarika) with the Interpretation of the Heart of Dependent Origination (Pratityasamutpadahrdayavyakhyana), by R.C. Jamieson (U.S. ed. N.Y.: Peter Lang, 2002).

The Lankavatara Sutra: A Mahayana Text. Translated by Daisetz Teitaro Suzuki. Foreword by Moti Lal Pandit (New Delhi: Munshiram Manoharlal, 1999).

"The Sutra of Hui Neng", in *The Diamond Sutra and the Sutra of Hui Neng,* second section, pp. 55–156. Translated by A. F. Price and Wong Mou-Lam, foreword by W. Y. Evans-Wentz (Boston: Shambhala, 1990).

19. The "Perfect Practice" of Adidam unfolds in three stages (or phases), which Avatar Adi Da Samraj has epitomized in the three-part Admonition: (1) <u>Be</u> Consciousness (Itself), (2) "Contemplate" Consciousness (Itself), and (3) Transcend everything in Consciousness (Itself). The first and second stages of the "Perfect Practice" are the foundation on which the third stage of the "Perfect Practice" (which is the Most Perfect Awakening to the seventh stage of life) can demonstrate itself.

20. For definitions of Avatar Adi Da's Names and Titles, see note 14 above.

When Avatar Adi Da describes that He is "the First, the Last, and the Only seventh stage Avataric Divine Realizer, Avataric Divine Revealer, and Avataric Divine Self-Revelation of Reality, Truth, and <u>Real</u> (Acausal) God", He is not making exclusive claims that Enlightenment is not possible for (apparent) others. Rather, He is describing His Very Divine Person and the unique Avataric Divine nature of His human Birth and Life-Demonstration. Once the seventh stage Way of Adidam has been Revealed in the cosmic domain, via His Avataric Divine Demonstration, it is not necessary for another to do so. However, any of Avatar Adi Da's devotees who Realizes the seventh stage Awakening will Awaken to and as His Perfect Divine Self-Condition, beyond all ego-presumptions of separateness and "difference".

Adidam—When Avatar Adi Da Samraj first Gave the name "Adidam" in January 1996, He pointed out that the final "m" adds a mantric force, evoking the effect of the primal Sanskrit syllable "Om". (For Avatar Adi Da's Revelation of the most profound esoteric significance of "Om" as the Divine Sound of His own Very Being, see *The Dawn Horse Testament*.) Simultaneously, the final "m" suggests the English word "Am" (expressing "I Am"), such that the Name "Adidam" also evokes Avatar Adi Da's Primal Self-Confession, "I Am Adi Da", or, more simply, "I Am Da" (or, in Sanskrit, "Aham Da Asmi").

Advaita Vedanta—Vedanta is the principal philosophical tradition of Hinduism. "Advaita" means "non-dual". Advaita Vedanta, then, is a philosophy of non-dualism. Its origins lie in the ancient esoteric Teaching that the Divine is the only Reality.

Amrita Nadi—Amrita Nadi is Sanskrit for "Channel (or Current, or Nerve) of Ambrosia (or Immortal Nectar)". Amrita Nadi is the ultimate "organ", or root-structure, of the body-mind, Realized as such (in Its "Regenerated" form) in the seventh stage of life in the Way of Adidam.

Avataric Divine Self-"Emergence". *See* **Divine Self-"Emergence", Avataric**.

"Bright"—By the word "Bright" (and its variations, such as "Brightness"), Avatar Adi Da refers to the Self-Existing and Self-Radiant Divine Reality that He has Revealed since His Birth. Avatar Adi Da Named His own Self-Evidently Divine Self-Condition "the 'Bright'" in His Infancy, as soon as He acquired the capability of language.

This term is placed in quotation marks to indicate that Avatar Adi Da uses it with the specific meaning described here.

causal (dimension)—*See* **gross, subtle, causal (dimensions)**.

the Circle—The Circle of the body-mind is a primary pathway of natural life-energy and the Divine Spirit-Energy in the body-mind. It is composed of two arcs: the descending Current, which flows through the frontal line—down the front of the body, from the crown of the head to the bodily base—and which corresponds to the gross dimension of the body-mind; and the ascending Current, which flows through the spinal line—up the back of the body, from the bodily base to the crown of the head—and which corresponds to the subtle dimension of the body-mind.

"create" / "Creator"—Avatar Adi Da Samraj places the word "create" (and its variants) in quotation marks when He wishes to indicate the sense of "so to speak"—Communicating that, in the Indivisible Unity of Reality, any particular "thing" is not truly (but only apparently) appearing "out of nothing" or being caused to appear (or "created").

"difference"—The root of the egoic presumption of separateness—in contrast with the Realization of Oneness, or Non-"Difference", Which is Native to the Divine Acausal Self-Condition. This term is placed in quotation marks to indicate that Avatar Adi Da uses it in the "so to speak" sense. He is Communicating (by means of the quotation marks) that, in Reality, there is no such thing as "difference", even though it appears to be the case from the "point of view" of ordinary human perception.

Divine Re-Awakening—For Avatar Adi Da's account of His Divine Re-Awakening, at the Vedanta Society Temple in Hollywood in September 1970, see chapter 16 in Part One of *The Knee Of Listening*.

Divine Self-"Emergence", Avataric—On January 11, 1986, Avatar Adi Da passed through a profound Yogic Swoon, Which He later described as the Yogic Establishment of His Avataric Divine Self-"Emergence". Avatar Adi Da's Avataric Divine Self-"Emergence" is an ongoing Process in which His Avatarically-Born bodily (human) Divine Form has been (and is ever more profoundly and potently being) conformed to Himself, the Very Divine Person, such that His bodily (human) Form is now (and forever hereafter) an utterly Unobstructed Sign and Agent of His own Divine Being. For Avatar Adi Da's extended description of His Avataric Divine Self-"Emergence", see Part Three of *The Knee Of Listening*.

Divine Self-Recognition—Divine Self-Recognition is the ego-transcending and world-transcending Intelligence of the Divine Acausal Self-Condition in relation to all conditional phenomena. The devotee of Avatar Adi Da who Realizes the seventh stage of life simply Abides as the Divine Conscious Light Itself, and he or she Freely Self-Recognizes (or inherently and instantly and most perfectly comprehends and perceives) all phenomena (including body, mind, conditional self, and conditional world) as transparent (or merely apparent), and un-necessary, and inherently non-binding modifications of the same "Bright" Conscious Light.

Divine Translation / Divinely Translate—Avatar Adi Da has Revealed that the Awakening to the seventh stage of life is not an "endpoint" but is (rather) the beginning of the final Spiritual process. One of the unique aspects of Avatar Adi Da's Revelation is His precise description of the seventh stage process as consisting of four phases: Divine Transfiguration, Divine Transformation, Divine Indifference, and Divine Translation.

The Final Sign (or Demonstration) Of The Only-By-Me Revealed and Given Seventh Stage Of Life (and Of The Total Practice Of The Only-By-Me Revealed and Given "Radical" Way Of The Heart) Is The Great Event Of Divine Translation—Which Is . . . The Process Of Transition To (or "Dawning" As) My Divine Self-Domain Via The Divinely "Bright" Outshining Of The Cosmic Domain In The Only-By-Me Revealed and Given Divine Sphere and Sign Of The "Midnight Sun" (Most Perfectly Beyond and Prior To all-and-All Of Cosmic, or conditional, forms, beings, signs, conditions, relations, and things).

—Avatar Adi Da Samraj
The Dawn Horse Testament

ego-"I"—The fundamental activity of self-contraction, or the presumption of separate and separative existence.

The "I" is placed in quotation marks to indicate that it is used by Avatar Adi Da in the "so to speak" sense. He is Communicating (by means of the quotation marks) that, in Reality, there is no such thing as the separate "I", even though it appears to be the case from the "point of view" of ordinary human perception.

frontal line—The frontal line is the subtle energy-pathway in the human structure (extending from the crown of the head to the bodily base) through which both the natural life-energy and the Divine Spirit-Energy flow downward (or in a descending direction).

Great Tradition—The "Great Tradition" is Avatar Adi Da's term for the total inheritance of human, cultural, religious, magical, mystical, Spiritual, and Transcendental paths, philosophies, and testimonies, from all the eras and cultures of humanity—which inheritance has (in the present era of worldwide communication) become the common legacy of humankind.

gross, subtle, causal (dimensions)—Avatar Adi Da (in agreement with certain esoteric schools in the Great Tradition) describes conditional existence as having three fundamental dimensions—gross, subtle, and causal.

"Gross" means "made up of material (or physical) elements". The gross (or physical) dimension is, therefore, associated with the physical body. The gross dimension is also associated with experience in the waking state and, as Avatar Adi Da Reveals, with the frontal line of the body-mind and with the left side of the heart (or the gross physical heart).

The subtle dimension, which is senior to and pervades the gross dimension, consists of the etheric (or personal life-energy) functions, the lower mental functions (including the conscious mind, the subconscious mind, and the unconscious mind) and higher mental functions (of discriminative mind, mentally presumed egoity, and will), and is associated with experience in the dreaming state. In the human psycho-physical structure, the subtle dimension is primarily associated with the middle station of the heart (or the heart chakra), the spinal line, the brain core, and the subtle centers of mind in the higher brain.

The causal dimension is senior to both the gross and the subtle dimensions. It is the root of attention, or the root-sense of existence as a separate self. The causal dimension is associated with the right side of the heart, specifically with the sinoatrial node, or "pacemaker" (the psycho-physical source of the heartbeat). Its corresponding state of consciousness is the formless awareness of deep sleep.

hearing—*See* **listening, hearing, seeing**.

Kundalini Yoga—A tradition of Yogic techniques in which practice is devoted to awakening the internal energy processes, which bring about subtle experiences and blisses. But, as Avatar Adi Da has indicated, the true manifestation of Spiritual Awakening is spontaneous, a Grace Given in the Company of a True Siddha-Guru, and in the midst of an entire life of practice in his or her Company.

Lineage-Gurus, Avatar Adi Da's— The principal Spiritual Masters who served Avatar Adi Da Samraj during His "Sadhana Years" belong to a single Lineage of extraordinary Yogis, whose Parama-Guru (Supreme Guru) was the Divine "Goddess" (or "Mother-Shakti").

Swami Rudrananda (1928–1973), or Albert Rudolph (known as "Rudi"), was Avatar Adi Da's first human Teacher—from 1964 to 1968, in New York City. Rudi served Avatar Adi Da Samraj in the development of basic practical life-disciplines and the frontal Yoga, which is the process whereby knots and obstructions in the physical and etheric dimensions of the body-mind are penetrated, opened, surrendered, and released through Spiritual reception in the frontal line of the body-mind. Rudi's own Teachers included Swami Muktananda (with whom Rudi studied for many years) and Bhagavan Nityananda (the Indian Adept-Realizer who was also Swami Muktananda's Guru). Rudi met Bhagavan Nityananda shortly before Bhagavan Nityananda's death, and Rudi always thereafter acknowledged Bhagavan Nityananda as his original and principal Guru.

The second Teacher in Avatar Adi Da's Lineage of Blessing was Swami Muktananda (1908–1982), who was born in Mangalore, South India. Having left home at the age of fifteen, he wandered for many years, seeking the Divine Truth from sources all over India. Eventually, he came under the Spiritual Influence of Bhagavan Nityananda, whom he recognized as his Guru and in whose Spiritual Company he mastered Kundalini Yoga. Swami Muktananda served Avatar Adi Da as Guru during the period from 1968 to 1970. In the summer of 1969, during Avatar Adi Da's second visit to India, Swami Muktananda wrote a letter confirming Avatar Adi Da's attainment of "Yogic Liberation", and acknowledging His right to Teach others. However, from the beginning of their relationship, Swami

Muktananda instructed Avatar Adi Da to visit Bhagavan Nityananda's burial site every day (whenever Avatar Adi Da was at Swami Muktananda's Ashram in Ganeshpuri, India) as a means to surrender to Bhagavan Nityananda as the Supreme Guru of the Lineage.

Bhagavan Nityananda, a great Yogi of South India, was Avatar Adi Da's third Guru. Little is known about the circumstances of Bhagavan Nityananda's birth and early life, although it is said that even as a child he showed the signs of a Realized Yogi. It is also known that he abandoned conventional life as a boy and wandered as a renunciate. Many miracles (including spontaneous healings) and instructive stories are attributed to him. Bhagavan Nityananda surrendered the body on August 8, 1961. Although He did not meet Bhagavan Nityananda in the flesh, Avatar Adi Da enjoyed Bhagavan Nityananda's direct Spiritual Influence from the subtle plane, and He acknowledges Bhagavan Nityananda as a direct and principal Source of Spiritual Instruction during His years with Swami Muktananda.

On His third visit to India, while visiting Bhagavan Nityananda's burial shrine, Avatar Adi Da was instructed by Bhagavan Nityananda to relinquish all others as Guru and to surrender directly to the Divine Goddess in Person as Guru. Thus, Bhagavan Nityananda passed Avatar Adi Da to the Divine Goddess Herself, the Parama-Guru (or Source-Guru) of the Lineage that included Bhagavan

Nityananda, Swami Muktananda, and Rudi.

Avatar Adi Da's "Sadhana Years" came to an end in the Great Event of His Divine Re-Awakening, when Avatar Adi Da Realized His Inherent Oneness with the Divine Goddess (thereby ceasing to relate to Her as His Guru).

Avatar Adi Da's full account of His "Sadhana Years" is Given in Part One of *The Knee Of Listening*. Avatar Adi Da's description of His "Relationship" to the Divine "Goddess" is Given in "I Am The Icon Of Unity", in *He-and-She Is Me*.

listening, hearing, seeing—
Avatar Adi Da describes the entire course of the Way of Adidam as falling into four primary phases:

1. listening to Him

2. hearing Him

3. seeing Him

4. the "Perfect Practice" of Identifying with Him

For a description of the unfolding phases of practice of Adidam, see *Adidam: The True World-Religion Given by the Promised God-Man, Adi Da Samraj* and *The Dawn Horse Testament*.

"Listening" is Avatar Adi Da's technical term for the beginning practice of the Way of Adidam. A listening devotee literally "listens" to Avatar Adi Da's Instruction and applies it in his or her life.

The core of the listening process (and of all future practice of the Way of Adidam) is the practice of Ruchira Avatara Bhakti Yoga (or turning the four principal faculties of the body-mind—body, emotion, mind, and breath—to Him)—supported by practice of the "conscious process" and "conductivity" and by the embrace of the functional, practical, relational, and cultural disciplines Given by Him.

It is during the listening phase (once the foundation practice is fully established) that the devotee applies to come on extended formal retreat in Avatar Adi Da's physical Company (or, after His physical Lifetime, in the physical company, and the by-Him-Spiritually-Empowered circumstances, of the Ruchira Sannyasin Order of Adidam Ruchiradam). In the retreat circumstance, when the rightly prepared devotee truly (whole bodily) turns the principal faculties to Him, Avatar Adi Da is spontaneously Moved to Grant His Spiritual Initiation (or Ruchira Shaktipat), such that the devotee can become more and more consistently capable of tangibly receiving His Spiritual Transmission. This is the beginning of the Spiritually Awakened practice of the Way of Adidam—when the devotional relationship to Avatar Adi Da becomes (by His Divine Spiritual Grace) the devotional-and-Spiritual relationship to Him.

The phase of listening to Avatar Adi Da, rightly and effectively engaged, eventually culminates (by His Divine Spiritual Grace) in the true hearing of Him. The devotee has begun to hear Avatar Adi Da when there is most fundamental understanding of the root-act of egoity (or self-contraction), or the unique capability to consistently transcend the self-contraction. The capability of true hearing is not something the ego can "achieve". That capability can only be Granted, by Means of Avatar Adi Da's Divine Spiritual Grace, to His devotee who has effectively completed the (eventually, Spiritually Awakened) process of listening.

When Spiritually Awakened practice of the Way of Adidam is magnified by means of the hearing-capability, the devotee has the necessary preparation to (in due course) engage that Spiritually Awakened practice in the "fully technically responsible" manner. This is another point (in the course of the Way of Adidam) when the devotee engages an extended formal retreat in Avatar Adi Da's physical Company (or, after His physical Lifetime, in the physical company, and the by-Him-Spiritually-Empowered circumstances, of the Ruchira Sannyasin Order of Adidam Ruchiradam). In this case, in Response to the devotee's more mature practice of devotional and Spiritual resort to Him, Avatar Adi Da Gives the Initiatory Spiritual Gift of Upward-turned Spiritual receptivity of Him (as He describes in *Hridaya Rosary*). This is Avatar Adi Da's Spiritual Initiation of His devotee into the seeing phase of practice, which Avatar Adi Da describes as the "fully technically responsible" form of Spiritually Awakened resort to Him.

One of the principal signs of the transition from the listening-hearing practice to the both-hearing-_and_-seeing practice is emotional conversion from the reactive emotions that characterize egoic self-obsession, to the open-hearted, Radiant Happiness that characterizes fully technically responsible Spiritual devotion to Avatar Adi Da. This true and stable emotional conversion coincides with stable Upward-to-Him-turned receptivity of Avatar Adi Da's Spiritual Transmission.

As the process of seeing develops, the body-mind becomes more and more fully Infused by Avatar Adi Da's Spirit-Baptism, purified of any psycho-physical patterning that _diminishes_ that reception. With increasing maturity in the seeing process, Avatar Adi Da's Transmission of the "Bright" is experienced in the unique form that He describes as "the 'Thumbs'"—and, through this process, the devotee is gracefully grown entirely beyond identification with the body-mind. The seeing process is complete when the devotee receives Avatar Adi Da's Gift of Spiritually Awakening as the Witness-Consciousness (That Stands Prior to body, mind, and world, and even the act of attention itself). This Awakening to the Witness-Consciousness marks readiness for another period of Initiatory retreat in Avatar Adi Da's physical Company (or, after His physical Lifetime, in the physical company, and the by-Him-Spiritually-Empowered circumstances, of the Ruchira Sannyasin Order of Adidam Ruchiradam), in which He Spiritually Initiates the devotee into the "Perfect Practice".

"Midnight Sun"—A term Avatar Adi Da uses to refer to His Revelation of the esoteric visionary representation of Reality as a White Sphere in a black field—which Sphere is His own Divine Form.

Avatar Adi Da places this term in quotation marks to indicate that He uses it with the specific technical meaning described here (rather than any other more common general meaning).

Most Perfect / Most Ultimate—Avatar Adi Da uses the phrase "Most Perfect(ly)" in the sense of "Absolutely Perfect(ly)". Similarly, the phrase "Most Ultimate(ly)" is equivalent to "Absolutely Ultimate(ly)". "Most Perfect(ly)" and "Most Ultimate(ly)" are always references to the seventh (or Divinely Enlightened) stage of life. "Perfect(ly)" and "Ultimate(ly)" (without "Most") refer to the practice and Realization in the context of the "Perfect Practice" of the Way of Adidam (or, when Avatar Adi Da is making reference to the Great Tradition, to practice and Realization in the context of the sixth stage of life).

mudra—Gesture of the hands, face, or body that outwardly expresses a state of ecstasy. Avatar Adi Da sometimes spontaneously exhibits mudras as Signs of His Blessing and Purifying Work with His devotees and the world.

muladhar—The chakra (or energy-center) associated with the bodily base.

"Perfect Practice"—The "Perfect Practice" is Avatar Adi Da's technical term for the discipline of the most mature stages of practice in the Way of Adidam. The "Perfect Practice" is practice in the Domain of Consciousness Itself (as opposed to practice from the "point of view" of the body or the mind). The "Perfect Practice" unfolds in three phases, the third of which is Divine Enlightenment. This term is placed in quotation marks to indicate that Avatar Adi Da uses it with the specific technical meaning described here.

Perfect (or "Radical") Self-Manifestation of the "Thumbs"—*See* **Samadhi of the "Thumbs"**.

Perfectly Subjective—Avatar Adi Da uses this phrase to describe the True Divine Source (or "Subject") of the conditionally manifested worlds—as opposed to regarding the Acausal Divine as some sort of objective "Other". Thus, in the phrase "Perfectly Subjective", the word "Subjective" does not have the sense of "relating to the inward experience of an individual", but, rather, it has the sense of "Being Consciousness Itself, the True 'Subject' of all apparent experience".

"Point of View"—In Avatar Adi Da's Wisdom-Teaching, "Point of View" is in quotation marks and capitalized when referring to the "Position" of Consciousness Itself, Prior to (and independent of) the body-mind or conditional existence altogether. The "Point of View" of Consciousness Itself is the basis of the "Perfect Practice" of the Way of Adidam.

"radical"—Derived from the Latin "radix", meaning "root". Thus, "radical" principally means "irreducible", "fundamental", or "relating to the origin". Thus, Avatar Adi Da defines "radical" as "at-the-root". Because Adi Da Samraj uses "radical" in this literal sense, it appears in quotation marks in His Wisdom-Teaching, in order to distinguish His usage from the common reference to an extreme (often political) view.

"Radical" Self-Manifestation of the "Thumbs". *See* **Samadhi of the "Thumbs"**.

"radical" self-understanding—Avatar Adi Da uses the word "understanding" to mean "the process of transcending egoity". Thus, to "understand" is to simultaneously observe the activity of the self-contraction and to surrender that activity via devotional resort to Him.

Avatar Adi Da has Revealed that, despite their intention to Realize Reality (or Truth, or Real Acausal God), all religious and Spiritual traditions (other than the Way of Adidam) are involved, in one manner or another (relating to either the subtle or the causal dimension of existence), with the search to satisfy the ego. Only Avatar Adi Da has Revealed the Way to "radically" understand the ego and (in due course, through intensive formal practice of the

Way of Adidam, as His formally acknowledged devotee) to most perfectly transcend the ego.

Ramana Maharshi—Ramana Maharshi (1879–1950) is regarded by many as the greatest Indian Sage of the twentieth century. Following a spontaneous death-like event as a teenager, he abandoned home for a life of Spiritual practice. Eventually, an ashram was established around him at Tiruvannamalai in South India, which still exists today.

Rang Avadhoot—*See* **Lineage-Gurus, Avatar Adi Da's**.

Real (Acausal) God—The True (and Perfectly Subjective) Source of all conditions, the True and Spiritual Divine Person—rather than any ego-made (and, thus, false, or limited) presumption about God.

Ruchira Avatara Bhakti Yoga—Ruchira Avatara Bhakti Yoga is the principal Gift, Calling, and Discipline Offered by Avatar Adi Da Samraj to His devotees.

The phrase "Ruchira Avatara Bhakti Yoga" is itself a summary of the Way of Adidam. "Bhakti", in Sanskrit, is "love, adoration, or devotion", while "Yoga" is "God-Realizing discipline" (or "practice"). "Ruchira Avatara Bhakti Yoga" is, thus, "the practice of devotion to the Ruchira Avatar, Adi Da Samraj".

The practice of Ruchira Avatara Bhakti Yoga is the process of turning the four principal facul-ties (body, emotion, mind, and breath) to Avatar Adi Da (in and <u>as</u> His Avatarically-Born bodily human Divine Form) in every moment and under all circumstances.

Rudi—*See* **Lineage-Gurus, Avatar Adi Da's**.

"Sadhana Years"—The period of time in Avatar Adi Da's early Life, starting when He, most intensively, began His Quest to recover the Truth of Existence (at Columbia College) in 1957 and ending with His Divine Re-Awakening in 1970. Avatar Adi Da's full description of His "Sadhana Years" is Given in *The Knee Of Listening*.

The term "Sadhana Years" is placed in quotation marks to indicate that it is used by Avatar Adi Da in the "so to speak" sense. In this case, it indicates that, because of the Avataric Divine Nature of His Birth and Life, Avatar Adi Da's years of apparent "sadhana" were actually part of His Submission to humankind and preparation of the vehicle of His Body-Mind to Teach and Bless. Avatar Adi Da Samraj intentionally engaged His "Sadhana Years" as the Process of "Learning Humankind". As the Avatarically Incarnate (and Inherently egoless) Divine Person, there was no other necessity for Him to engage any form of apparent "sadhana", because there was (in His Case) no egoity to be purified and tran-scended.

"Sahaja Nirvikalpa Samadhi"—The Sanskrit word "Samadhi" tradi-tionally denotes various exalted states that appear in the context of esoteric meditation and Realization. The Sanskrit term "Nirvikalpa Samadhi" literally means "meditative ecstasy without form", or "deep meditative concentration (or absorption) in which there is no perception of form (or defined experiential content)". "Sahaja" is Sanskrit for "born together, innate, or natural". Thus, "Sahaja Nirvikalpa Samadhi" means "Innate Samadhi without form". As Avatar Adi Da notes in His Essay "'God'-Talk, Real-God-Realization, Most Perfect Divine Self-Awakening, and the Seven Possible Stages of Life", the fourth, fifth, sixth, and seventh stages of life each have a characteristic mode of "Sahaja Nirvikalpa Samadhi". Avatar Adi Da's full description of seventh stage Sahaja Nirvikalpa Samadhi is Given in *The Dawn Horse Testament Of The Ruchira Avatar.*

sahasrar—In the traditional system of seven chakras, the sahasrar is the highest chakra (or subtle energy-center), associated with the crown of the head and above.

The sahasrar is described as a "thousand-petaled lotus", the terminal of Light to which the Yogic process (of Spiritual ascent through the chakras) aspires. However, in *The Knee Of Listening*, Avatar Adi Da describes how He spontaneously experienced what He calls the "severing of the sahasrar". The Spirit-Energy no longer ascended into the crown of the head (and beyond), nor was confined to the structure of the chakras.

Samadhi of the "Thumbs"—"The 'Thumbs'" is Avatar Adi Da's technical term for the Invasion of the body-mind by a particular form of the forceful Descent of His Divine Spirit-Current.

In the fullest form of this experience, which Avatar Adi Da calls "the Samadhi of the 'Thumbs'", His Spirit-Invasion Descends all the way to the bottom of the frontal line of the body-mind (at the bodily base) and ascends through the spinal line, overwhelming the ordinary human sense of bodily existence, infusing the whole being with intense blissfulness, and releasing the ordinary, confined sense of body, mind, and separate self. Eventually, in what Avatar Adi Da calls the "'Radical' Self-Manifestation of the 'Thumbs'", this process leads to the stable awakening of the Witness-Consciousness and the transition to the "Perfect Practice" of Adidam.

Avatar Adi Da's Revelation-Gift of the "Thumbs" is unique to the Way of Adidam, for it is a specific manifestation of the "Crashing Down" (or the Divine Descent) of Avatar Adi Da's Spirit-Baptism, into the body-minds of His devotees. The Samadhi of the "Thumbs" is a kind of "Nirvikalpa" (or formless) Samadhi—but in descent in the frontal line, rather than in ascent in the spinal line.

searchless Beholding (of Avatar Adi Da)—The primary practice of the Way of Adidam, which begins after the foundation preparation is established and Avatar Adi Da has been moved to Grant Divine

Spiritual Initiation to His devotee (in the context of extended formal retreat in His physical Company—or, after His physical Lifetime, in the physical company, and the by-Him-Spiritually-Empowered circumstances, of the Ruchira Sannyasin Order of Adidam Ruchiradam). The practice of searchlessly Beholding Avatar Adi Da is the Beholding of His Avatarically-Born bodily (human) Divine Form, free of any seeking-effort, and the searchless reception of His Spiritual Transmission.

Self-Existing and Self-Radiant—"Self-Existing" and "Self-Radiant" are terms describing the two fundamental aspects of the One Divine Person (or Reality)—Existence (or Being, or Consciousness) Itself, and Radiance (or Energy, or Light) Itself.

Self-Recognition. *See* **Divine Self-Recognition**.

Shakti—A Sanskrit term for the Divinely Manifesting Spiritual Energy, Spiritual Power, or Spirit-Current of the Divine Person.

spinal line—The spinal line is the subtle energy-pathway in the human structure (extending from the bodily base to the crown of the head) through which both the natural life-energy and the Divine Spirit-Energy flow upward (or in an ascending direction). Many traditional Yogas espouse mystical ascent via the spinal line and the brain core.

subtle (dimension)—*See* **gross, subtle, causal (dimensions)**.

Swami Muktananda—*See* **Lineage-Gurus, Avatar Adi Da's**.

Swami Nityananda—*See* **Lineage-Gurus, Avatar Adi Da's**.

the "Thumbs"—From time to time throughout His early Life, Avatar Adi Da experienced the forceful Spiritual Descent of the "Bright" into His body-mind. He describes it as feeling like "a mass of gigantic thumbs coming down from above". Therefore, just as He named His Divine State "the 'Bright'" as a child, He also, in childhood, gave a name to the Descent of the "Bright"—"the 'Thumbs'". This manifestation of the "Thumbs" is one of the unique Spiritual signs associated with Avatar Adi Da's Appearance. Once they have become fully technically responsible for the reception of Avatar Adi Da's Spiritual Blessing-Transmission, His devotees (in due course) experience this unique (and uniquely life-transforming) manifestation of His Spiritual Descent as a Gift Given by Him. See *The Dawn Horse Testament*.

Avatar Adi Da's Gift of the "Thumbs" is what makes it possible to enter the most mature stages of Adidam—the "Perfect Practice". *See also* **Samadhi of the "Thumbs"**.

Witness / Witness-Consciousness / Witness-Position—When Consciousness is Free of identification with the body-mind, It Stands in Its natural "Position" as the Conscious Witness of all that arises to and in and as the body-mind.

In the Way of Adidam, the stable Realization of the Witness-Position is a Spiritual Gift from Avatar Adi Da, made possible by (and necessarily following upon) the reception of His Spiritual Gift of the "Thumbs". The stable Realization of the Witness-Position is the characteristic of the first stage of the "Perfect Practice". See *The Dawn Horse Testament*.

The Avataric Great Sage,
ADI DA SAMRAJ

Become a Formal Devotee of Avatar Adi Da Samraj

In the depth of every human being, there is a profound need for answers to the fundamental questions of existence. Is there a God? What is beyond this life? Why is there suffering? What is Truth? What is Reality?

In this book, you have been introduced to the Wisdom-Revelation of Avatar Adi Da, whose Teachings truly and completely address all of these fundamental questions. How can Avatar Adi Da resolve these fundamental questions? Because He speaks, not from the "point of view" of the human dilemma, but directly from the unique Freedom of His Divine State. Adi Da's Birth in 1939 was an intentional embrace of the human situation, for the sake of Revealing the Way of Divine Liberation to all and Offering the Spiritual Blessing that carries beings to that true Freedom. He is thus the fulfillment of the ancient intuitions of the "Avatar"—the One Who Appears in human Form, as a direct manifestation of the Unmanifest Reality.

Through a 28-year process of Teaching-Work (beginning in 1972), Avatar Adi Da established the Way of Adidam—the Way of the devotional and Spiritual relationship to Him. In those years of Teaching, He spoke for many hours with groups of His devotees—always looking for them, as representatives of humanity, to ask all of their questions about God, Truth, Reality, and human life. In response, He Gave the ecstatic Way of heart-Communion with Him, and all the details of how that process unfolds. Thus, He created a new tradition, based on His direct Revelation (as Avatar) of the Divine Reality.

Avatar Adi Da Samraj does not offer you a set of beliefs, or even a set of Spiritual techniques. He simply Offers you His Revelation of Truth as a Free Gift. If you are moved to take up His Way, He invites you to enter into an extraordinarily deep and transformative devotional and Spiritual relationship to Him. On the following pages, we present a number of ways that you can choose to deepen your response to Adi Da Samraj and consider becoming His formal devotee.

To find Avatar Adi Da Samraj is to find the Very Heart of Reality—tangibly felt in your own heart as the Deepest Truth of Existence. This is the great mystery that you are invited to discover. ■

Adidam is not a conventional religion.
    Adidam is not a conventional way of life.
        Adidam is about the transcending of the ego-"I".
Adidam is about the Freedom of Divine Self-Realization.

Adidam is not based on mythology or belief.
Adidam is a "reality practice".
Adidam is a "reality consideration", in which the various modes of egoity are progressively transcended.

Adidam is a universally applicable Way of life.
Adidam is for those who will choose It, and whose hearts and intelligence fully respond to Me and My Offering.
Adidam is a Great Revelation, and It is to be freely and openly communicated to all.

AVATAR ADI DA SAMRAJ

For what you can do next to respond to Avatar Adi Da's Offering, or to simply find out more about Him and the Way of Adidam, please use the information given in the following pages.

Contact an Adidam center near you
for courses and events
(p. 154)

Visit our website: www.adidam.org
(p. 155)

For young people:
Join the Adidam Youth Fellowship
(p. 156)

Support Avatar Adi Da's Work
and the Way of Adidam
(p. 156)

Order other books and recordings
by and about Avatar Adi Da Samraj
(pp. 157–62)

Contact an Adidam center near you

■ To find out about becoming a formal devotee of Avatar Adi Da, and for information about upcoming courses, events, and seminars in your area:

AMERICAS
12040 North Seigler Road
Middletown, CA 95461 USA
1-707-928-4936

PACIFIC-ASIA
12 Seibel Road
Henderson
Auckland 1008
New Zealand
64-9-838-9114

AUSTRALIA
P.O. Box 244
Kew 3101
Victoria
**1800 ADIDAM
(1800-234-326)**

EUROPE-AFRICA
Annendaalderweg 10
6105 AT Maria Hoop
The Netherlands
31 (0)20 468 1442

THE UNITED KINGDOM
uk@adidam.org
0845-330-1008

INDIA
Shree Love-Ananda Marg
Rampath, Shyam Nagar Extn.
Jaipur–302 019, India
91 (141) 2293080

E-MAIL:
correspondence@adidam.org

■ For more contact information about local Adidam groups, please see **www.adidam.org/centers**

Visit our website:
www.adidam.org

■ **SEE AUDIO-VISUAL PRESENTATIONS** on the Divine Life and Spiritual Revelation of Avatar Adi Da Samraj

■ **LISTEN TO DISCOURSES** Given by Avatar Adi Da Samraj to His practicing devotees—

- Transcending egoic notions of God
- Why Reality cannot be grasped by the mind
- How the devotional relationship to Avatar Adi Da moves you beyond ego-bondage
- The supreme process of Spiritual Transmission

■ **READ QUOTATIONS** from the "Source-Texts" of Avatar Adi Da Samraj—

- Real God as the <u>only</u> Reality
- The ancient practice of Guru-devotion
- The two opposing life-strategies characteristic of the West and the East—and the way beyond both
- The Prior Unity at the root of all that exists
- The limits of scientific materialism
- The true religion beyond all seeking
- The esoteric structure of the human being
- The real process of death and reincarnation
- The nature of Divine Enlightenment

■ **SUBSCRIBE** to the online *Adidam Revelation* magazine

For young people:
Join the Adidam Youth Fellowship

■ Young people under 21 can participate in the "Adidam Youth Fellowship"—either as a "friend" or practicing member. Adidam Youth Fellowship members participate in study programs, retreats, celebrations, and other events with other young people responding to Avatar Adi Da. To learn more about the Youth Fellowship, call or write:

Vision of Mulund Institute (VMI)
10336 Loch Lomond Road, PMB 146
Middletown, CA 95461
phone: (707) 928-6932
e-mail: vmi@adidam.org
www.visionofmulund.org

Support Avatar Adi Da's Work
and the Way of Adidam

■ If you are moved to serve Avatar Adi Da's Spiritual Work specifically through advocacy and/or financial patronage, please contact:

Advocacy
12180 Ridge Road
Middletown, CA 95461
phone: (707) 928-5267
e-mail: adidam_advocacy@adidam.org

Order other books and recordings by and about Avatar Adi Da Samraj

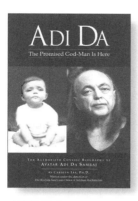

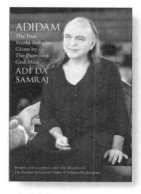

ADI DA

The Promised God-Man Is Here

The biography of Avatar Adi Da from His Birth to present time. Includes a wealth of quotations from His Writings and Talks, as well as stories told by His devotees. 358 pp., **$16.95**

ADIDAM

The True World-Religion Given by the Promised God-Man, Adi Da Samraj

A direct and simple summary of the fundamental aspects of the Way of Adidam. 196 pp., **$16.95**

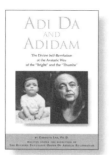

ADI DA AND ADIDAM

The Divine Self-Revelation of the Avataric Way of the "Bright" and the "Thumbs"

A brief introduction to Avatar Adi Da Samraj and His Unique Spiritual Revelation of the Way of Adidam. 64 pp., **$3.95**

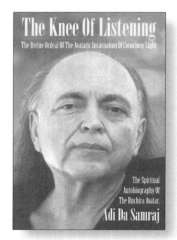

THE KNEE OF LISTENING

*The Divine Ordeal Of
The Avataric Incarnation
Of Conscious Light*

*The Spiritual Autobiography
Of The Ruchira Avatar,
Adi Da Samraj*

Born in 1939 on Long Island, New York, Adi Da Samraj describes His earliest life as an existence of constant and unmitigated Spiritual "Brightness". His observation, still in infancy, that others did not live in this manner led Him to undertake an awesome quest—to discover why human beings suffer and how they can transcend that suffering. His quest led Him to a confrontation with the bleak despair of post-industrial Godlessness, to a minute examination of the workings of subjective awareness, to discipleship in a lineage of profound Yogis, to a period of intense Christian mysticism, and finally to a Re-Awakening to the perfect state of "Brightness" He had known at birth.

In *The Knee Of Listening,* Avatar Adi Da also reveals His own direct awareness of His "deeper-personality vehicles"—the beings whose lives were the direct antecedents (or the "pre-history") of His present human lifetime—the great nineteenth-century Indian Realizers Sri Ramakrishna and Swami Vivekananda. Finally, Avatar Adi Da describes the series of profound transformational events that took place in the decades after His Divine Re-Awakening—each one a form of "Yogic death" for which there is no recorded precedent.

Altogether, *The Knee Of Listening* is the unparalleled history of how the Divine Conscious Light has Incarnated in human form, in order to grant everyone the possibility of Ultimate Divine Liberation, Freedom, and Happiness.

The Knee Of Listening *is without a doubt the most profound Spiritual autobiography of all time.*

—ROGER SAVOIE, PhD
philosopher; translator; author, *La Vipère et le Lion:
La Voie radicale de la Spiritualité*

822 pp., **$24.95**

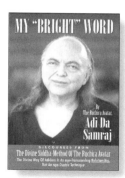

MY "BRIGHT" WORD

by Adi Da Samraj

New Edition of the Classic Spiritual Discourses originally published as *The Method of the Siddhas*

In these Talks from the early years of His Teaching-Work, Avatar Adi Da Gives extraordinary Instruction on the foundation of True Spiritual life, covering topics such as the primary mechanism by which we are preventing the Realization of Truth, the means to overcome this mechanism, and the true function of the Spiritual Master in relation to the devotee.

In modern language, this volume teaches the ancient all-time trans-egoic truths. It transforms the student by paradox and by example. Consciousness, understanding, and finally the awakened Self are the rewards. What more can anyone want?

—ELMER GREEN, PhD
Director Emeritus, Center for Applied Psychophysiology,
The Menninger Clinic

544 pp., **$24.95**

BUDDHISM, ADVAITISM, AND THE WAY OF ADIDAM

a Talk by Avatar Adi Da Samraj

Rather than being about egoity and seeking, the Way of Adidam is about the magnification of the understanding of egoity and its seeking. It is about a Revealed Process that directly transcends egoity in every moment, rather than merely at the end.

—AVATAR ADI DA SAMRAJ
June 21, 1995

In this remarkable Talk, Avatar Adi Da gives a unique summary of the ultimate Realizations in Buddhism and Advaitism (or Advaita Vedanta), and describes the sympathetic likenesses between these traditions and the Way of Adidam. Avatar Adi Da clarifies the uniqueness of the Way of Adidam, which is not based on strategically excluding conditional reality, but on transcending it.

CD, 5 Tracks, total running time: 55 minutes
$16.95

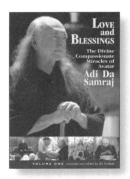

LOVE AND BLESSINGS
The Divine Compassionate Miracles of Avatar Adi Da Samraj

In *Love and Blessings—The Divine Compassionate Miracles of Avatar Adi Da Samraj*, twenty-five of His devotees tell heart-breaking stories of human need and Divine Response. A soldier in Iraq, a woman going blind in Holland, a son with his dying father in Australia, a woman with cancer in America—these and others tell how they asked Adi Da Samraj for His Blessing-Regard and of the miraculous process that ensued.

248 pp., **$19.95**

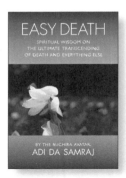

EASY DEATH
Spiritual Wisdom on the Ultimate Transcending of Death and Everything Else
by Adi Da Samraj

This new edition of *Easy Death* is thoroughly revised and updated with:

■ New Talks and Essays from Avatar Adi Da on death and ultimate transcendence

■ Accounts of profound Events of Yogic Death in Avatar Adi Da's own Life

■ Stories of His Blessing in the death transitions of His devotees

. . . an exciting, stimulating, and thought-provoking book that adds immensely to the ever-increasing literature on the phenomena of life and death. But, more important, perhaps, it is a confirmation that a life filled with love instead of fear can lead to ultimately meaningful life and death.

Thank you for this masterpiece.

—ELISABETH KÜBLER-ROSS, MD
author, *On Death and Dying*

544 pp., **$24.95**

The Adidam Revelation Discourses on DVD

In July of 2004, Adi Da Samraj began a series of Discourses that were broadcast live over the internet to all His devotees around the world. During these remarkable occasions, Adi Da Samraj answered questions from those who were present in the room with Him, but also from devotees in other parts of the world via speakerphone. The "Adidam Revelation Discourse" DVDs offer you the opportunity to see and hear Avatar Adi Da speak in these unique and intimate occasions of Divine Instruction to His devotees. Current available titles include:

TRANSCEND THE SELF-KNOT OF FEAR

Running time: 60 minutes. Includes subtitles in English, Spanish, French, German, Dutch, and Polish.

THE DIVINE IS NOT THE CAUSE

Running time: 72 minutes. Includes subtitles in English, Spanish, French, German, Dutch, Finnish, Polish, Czech, Chinese, Japanese, and Hebrew.

CRACKING THE CODE OF EXPERIENCE

Running time: 86 minutes. Includes subtitles in English, Spanish, German, Dutch, Polish, Czech, Chinese, Japanese, and Hebrew.

DVD, **$26.95** each.

The Five Books of the "Perfect Knowledge" Series

The books of the "Perfect Knowledge" Series are drawn from *Is: The "Perfect Knowledge" of Reality and The "Radical" Way to Realize It,* by the Avataric Great Sage, Adi Da Samraj. The five books of the "Perfect Knowledge" Series together comprise the complete text of *Is.*

THE PERFECT TRADITION

The Wisdom-Way of the Ancient Sages and Its Fulfillment in the Way of "Perfect Knowledge"

by The Avataric Great Sage, Adi Da Samraj

RELIGION AND REALITY

True Religion Is Not Belief in Any "God"-Idea but the Direct Experiential Realization of Reality Itself

by The Avataric Great Sage, Adi Da Samraj

THE LIBERATOR

The "Radical" Reality-Teachings of The Avataric Great Sage, Adi Da Samraj

THE ANCIENT REALITY-TEACHINGS

The Single Transcendental Truth Taught by the Great Sages of Buddhism and Advaitism— As Revealed by The Avataric Great Sage, Adi Da Samraj

THE WAY OF PERFECT KNOWLEDGE

The "Radical" Practice of Transcendental Spirituality in the Way of Adidam

by The Avataric Great Sage, Adi Da Samraj

The Avataric Divine Wisdom-Teaching
of Adi Da Samraj

The Avataric Divine Wisdom-Teaching of Adi Da Samraj is gathered together, in its final form, in the many "Source-Texts" which He has designated as His Eternal Communication to humankind. These "Source-Texts" are "True-Water-Bearers", or Bearers of the "True Water" of the "Bright" Divine Reality Itself.

Avatar Adi Da has grouped His "Source-Texts" into twenty-three "Streams", or "Courses". Each of these Courses conveys a particular aspect of His Avataric Divine Wisdom-Teaching—and each Course (other than the first) may, in principle, include any number of "Source-Texts".

The first Course is Avatar Adi Da's paramount "Source-Text", *The Dawn Horse Testament Of The Ruchira Avatar*. The remaining twenty-two Courses are divided into two groups: *The Heart Of The Adidam Revelation* (consisting of five Courses, which, together, present a comprehensive overview of Avatar Adi Da's entire Wisdom-Teaching) and *The Companions Of The True Dawn Horse* (consisting of seventeen Courses, each of which elaborates on particular topics from *The Dawn Horse Testament*).

> *The "Source-Texts"*
> *(or True-Water-Bearers)*
> *Of My Avataric Divine Wisdom-Teaching*
> *(In Its Twenty-Three Courses Of*
> *True-Water-Born Speech)—*
> *With [My] Divine Testament*
> *As The Epitome*
> *(or First and Principal Text,*
> *and "Bright" True-Water-Mill)*
> *Among Them—*
> *Are, Together, [My] Sufficient Word—*
> *Given, In Summary,*
> *To You*
> *(and, Therefore, To all).*
>
> —Avatar Adi Da Samraj
> *The Dawn Horse Testament*
> *Of The Ruchira Avatar*

The "Source-Texts" of the Avataric Divine Wisdom-Teaching of Adi Da Samraj (in Its Twenty-Three Courses)

The Dawn Horse Testament Of The Ruchira Avatar
(in Its Single Course)

THE DAWN HORSE TESTAMENT OF THE RUCHIRA AVATAR
The Testament Of Divine Secrets Of The Divine World-Teacher,
Ruchira Avatar Adi Da Samraj

The Heart Of The Adidam Revelation
(in Its Five Courses)

1. AHAM DA ASMI
   (BELOVED, I AM DA)
   The "Late-Time" Avataric Revelation Of The True and Spiritual
   Divine Person (The egoless Personal Presence Of Reality and Truth,
   Which Is The Only Real Acausal God)

2. RUCHIRA AVATARA GITA
   (THE AVATARIC WAY OF THE DIVINE HEART-MASTER)
   The "Late-Time" Avataric Revelation Of The Great Secret Of The Divinely Self-
   Revealed Way That Most Perfectly Realizes The True and Spiritual Divine
   Person (The egoless Personal Presence Of Reality and Truth,
   Which Is The Only Real Acausal God)

3. DA LOVE-ANANDA GITA
   (THE FREE AVATARIC GIFT OF THE DIVINE LOVE-BLISS)
   The "Late-Time" Avataric Revelation Of The Great Means To Worship and
   To Realize The True and Spiritual Divine Person (The egoless Personal Presence
   Of Reality and Truth, Which Is The Only Real Acausal God)

4. HRIDAYA ROSARY
   (FOUR THORNS OF HEART-INSTRUCTION)
   The "Late-Time" Avataric Revelation Of The Universally Tangible Divine
   Spiritual Body, Which Is The Supreme Agent Of The Great Means To Worship
   and To Realize The True and Spiritual Divine Person (The egoless Personal
   Presence Of Reality and Truth, Which Is The Only Real Acausal God)

5. ELEUTHERIOS
   (THE ONLY TRUTH THAT SETS THE HEART FREE)
   The "Late-Time" Avataric Revelation Of The "Perfect Practice" Of The Great
   Means To Worship and To Realize The True and Spiritual Divine Person
   (The egoless Personal Presence Of Reality and Truth, Which Is The Only
   Real Acausal God)

The Companions Of The True Dawn Horse
(in Their Seventeen Courses)

1. REAL (ACAUSAL) GOD IS THE INDIVISIBLE ONENESS OF UNBROKEN LIGHT
   *Reality, Truth, and The "Non-Creator" God In The Universal
   Transcendental Spiritual Way Of Adidam*

   THE TRANSMISSION OF DOUBT
   Transcending Scientific Materialism

2. THE TRULY HUMAN NEW WORLD-CULTURE OF UNBROKEN REAL-GOD-MAN
   *The Eastern Versus The Western Traditional Cultures Of Humankind,
   and The Unique New Non-Dual Culture Of The Universal
   Transcendental Spiritual Way Of Adidam*

   SCIENTIFIC PROOF OF THE EXISTENCE OF GOD WILL SOON BE ANNOUNCED
   BY THE WHITE HOUSE!
   *Prophetic Wisdom about the Myths and Idols of Mass Culture and Popular
   Religious Cultism, the New Priesthood of Scientific and Political Materialism,
   and the Secrets of Enlightenment Hidden in the Human Body*

   NOT-TWO IS PEACE
   The Ordinary People's Way of Global Cooperative Order

3. THE ONLY COMPLETE WAY TO REALIZE THE UNBROKEN LIGHT
   OF REAL (ACAUSAL) GOD
   *An Introductory Overview Of The "Radical" Divine Way Of
   The Universal Transcendental Spiritual Way Of Adidam*

4. THE KNEE OF LISTENING
   *The Divine Ordeal Of The Avataric Incarnation Of Conscious Light—
   The Spiritual Autobiography Of The Avataric Great Sage, Adi Da Samraj*

5. THE DIVINE SIDDHA-METHOD OF THE RUCHIRA AVATAR
   *The Divine Way Of Adidam Is An ego-Transcending Relationship,
   Not An ego-Centric Technique*

   Volume I: MY "BRIGHT" WORD

   Volume II: MY "BRIGHT" SIGHT

   Volume III: MY "BRIGHT" FORM

   Volume IV: MY "BRIGHT" ROOM

165

6. THE "FIRST ROOM" TRILOGY

BOOK ONE:
THE MUMMERY BOOK
A Parable Of Divine Tragedy, Told By Means Of
A Self-Illuminated Illustration Of The Totality Of Mind

BOOK TWO:
THE SCAPEGOAT BOOK
The Previously Secret Dialogue on the Avatarically Given Divine Way of
"Perfect-Knowledge"-Only, Once-Spoken in a Single Night of Conversation,
Between the Captive Divine Avatar and Great Sage, Raymond Darling, and
His Captor, the Great Fool, and False Teacher, and Notoriously Eccentric
Super-Criminal, Evelyn Disk—Herein Fully Given, Without Evelyn Disk's
Later and Famous and self-Serving Revisions, but Exactly As They Were
Originally Tape-Recorded, by Evelyn Disk himself, in the First Room, at the
State Mental Facility, near God's End, and Presented in Exact Accordance
with the Recent Revelatory and Complete Recounting, Given to the Waiting
World of Intelligent and Receptive Persons, by Meridian Smith, Who Was,
As Usual, Inexplicably Present

BOOK THREE:
THE HAPPENINE BOOK
The Childhood Teachings and The End-of-Childhood Revelations of The Famous
"Infant Sage", Raymond Darling—Compiled from Raymond Darling's
Original Handwritten Manuscripts, and Privately Held Tape-Recordings,
Discovered In The First Room By His True Servant-Devotee, Meridian Smith,
After The Miraculous Disappearance of The Avataric Great Sage

7. HE-AND-SHE IS ME
The Indivisibility Of Consciousness and Light In The Divine Body Of
The Ruchira Avatar

8. RUCHIRA SHAKTIPAT YOGA
The Divine (and Not Merely Cosmic) Spiritual Baptism In The Divine Way
Of Adidam

9. RUCHIRA TANTRA YOGA
The Physical-Spiritual (and Truly Religious) Method Of Mental, Emotional,
Sexual, and Whole Bodily Health and Enlightenment In The Divine Way
Of Adidam

EASY DEATH
Spiritual Wisdom on the Ultimate Transcending of Death and Everything Else

CONSCIOUS EXERCISE AND THE TRANSCENDENTAL SUN
The Universal ego-Transcending Principle of Love Applied to Exercise and
the Method of Common Physical Action—A Science of Whole Bodily Wisdom,
or True Emotion, Intended Most Especially for Those Engaged in Religious
(and, in Due Course, Spiritual) Life

We invite you to find out more about Avatar Adi Da Samraj and the Way of Adidam

■ Find out about our courses, seminars, events, and retreats by calling the regional center nearest you.

AMERICAS
12040 N. Seigler Rd.
Middletown, CA
95461 USA
1-707-928-4936

THE UNITED KINGDOM
uk@adidam.org
0845-330-1008

EUROPE-AFRICA
Annendaalderweg 10
6105 AT Maria Hoop
The Netherlands
31 (0)20 468 1442

PACIFIC-ASIA
12 Seibel Road
Henderson
Auckland 1008
New Zealand
64-9-838-9114

AUSTRALIA
P.O. Box 244
Kew 3101
Victoria
**1800 ADIDAM
(1800-234-326)**

INDIA
Shree Love-Ananda Marg
Rampath, Shyam Nagar Extn.
Jaipur–302 019, India
91 (141) 2293080

E-MAIL: **correspondence@adidam.org**

■ Order books, tapes, CDs, DVDs, and videos by and about Avatar Adi Da Samraj.
   1-877-770-0772 (from within North America)
   1-707-928-6653 (from outside North America)
   order online: **www.dawnhorsepress.com**

■ Visit us online:
   www.adidam.org
   Explore the online community of Adidam and discover more about Avatar Adi Da and the Way of Adidam.